FIFTH WEDNESDAY
JOURNAL

Defining literature. In real context.

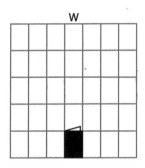

FIFTH WEDNESDAY
■ JOURNAL

Defining literature. In real context.
www.fifthwednesdayjournal.org

FALL 2009 • ISSUE 5

GUEST FICTION EDITOR
Bret Anthony Johnston

GUEST POETRY EDITOR
Laurence Lieberman

PUBLISHER AND EDITOR
Vern Miller

ART EDITOR AND DESIGNER
Jenn Hollmeyer

COPY EDITOR
LeAnn Spencer

ADVISORY EDITOR
James Ballowe

BOOK REVIEWS EDITOR
Daniel Libman

ASSISTANT EDITORS
Dale Barrigar   Monica Berlin
Kelly Davio   Christine Davis
Adam Gallari   Rachel Hall
Ixtaccihuatl   Susen James
Kristin LaTour   Terry Lucas
Susan Azar Porterfield   Brian Ray
Natania Rosenfeld   Ruan Wright

WEB EDITOR
George Yanos

TABLE OF CONTENTS

EDITOR'S NOTES

Dear Reader,

The editor's notes are just that — notes about the literary content, notes about the writers and artists represented, notes about the events and conditions important to the success of the enterprise, and notes that invite the wider community to become active partners. This issue continues our mission to make accessible the best writing and photography we can gather for our readers; it also marks a new beginning for *Fifth Wednesday Journal* as a recognized independent nonprofit organization devoted to the advancement of the literary and photographic arts as essential elements of American culture and to the artists who create the works in our pages.

Each year FWJ editors seek to recognize and reward the work of our contributing artists with the Editor's Prize in the categories of short fiction, poetry, and photography selected from works we have published in the previous fall and spring issues. This year we are fortunate to have three excellent independent judges for this difficult task. Our thanks go to Anna Leahy, Keith Gandal, and Barbara DeGenevieve who agreed to lend FWJ their expertise and time as judges. We are happy to announce their choices elsewhere in these pages. It is worth noting that the judge in each category had difficulty in separating just one work for recognition. Two judges decided to name two honorable mentions and one named co-winners. It is the job of editors and judges to find and encourage artists who use their talents and tools to create different styles and manners of addressing their themes and telling their stories. The decisions of the judges illustrate not only these different styles and manners, they also demonstrate the success of the editors in their selections.

Our guest poetry editor Laurence Lieberman and our guest fiction editor Bret Anthony Johnston have filled these pages with excellent reading. The editors of FWJ take great pleasure in bringing to our readers a sample of the talent that won Elizabeth Strout the Pulitzer Prize in Fiction in 2009. We are happy to offer the work of our feature poet, Michael Van Walleghen. James Ballowe's interview with him will make not only Mr. Van Walleghen's poetry, but all poetry more accessible to and more fun for everyone who reads it. And that's not all we have for our readers. Can anyone read Ira Wood's essay, "You Are What You Owe," and say they didn't laugh while learning what publishing, especially small press publishing, is like? The story of Ishi — "America's Last Natural Man" by Stephen Thomas — is a genuine piece of American history.

The poems and prose in this issue reflect in a large measure the styles and themes of interest to writers working in America today. Dave Smith, Peter Serchuk, Jonathan Liebson, and other established writers fully meet the expectations we have of them. They challenge us and inform us while they entertain us. We are always excited when we find among the manuscripts sent to us work by an emerging writer that we can present to our readers with pride. And this issue is no exception. I know all our readers will enjoy the work of Samira Grace Didos, Stephen Thomas, and Ryan Mecklenburg. The backgrounds and lives of the writers are as varied as their works. An important part of a literary magazine is the contributors' notes at the back. Please go there to find the author's profile for every work in our pages. You will meet most of them again somewhere in the literary scene of this country.

Publishing the print magazine is only part of what we want to accomplish. Our tagline — *Defining literature. In real context.* — is intended to describe our intention to bring the stories, poems, and photographs in these pages to a broader community through readings and other programs open to the public. Projects aimed at this goal have been discussed and now await funding opportunities for their realization. Like most literary publications, we are faced with the additional challenge of how to best utilize the opportunities offered by the Internet and electronic transfer of writing and photography. Whatever our decisions in this area, we face expanded costs. To bridge the gap between costs and revenues provided by subscriptions and sales of the magazine, we must rely on donations by individuals who support our mission. In June, we were informed that the Internal Revenue Service had approved our application for status as a 501(c)(3) organization under the IRS Tax Code. Donations in support of our mission are now tax exempt to the fullest extent of the law. We are hopeful our tax exempt status will add to the incentive to join us in sharing the work of America's artists and poets with as many as we can reach.

One final note. There are five new names on our masthead for this issue. Christine Davis, Adam Gallari, Kristin LaTour, Terry Lucas, and Brian Ray have added their considerable talent and hard work to our team of editors. Our readers can find a brief biography for each of them on our website.

— *Vern Miller*
Publisher and Editor

EDITOR'S PRIZES

POETRY

Our choice for poetry is **Ray Gonzalez** for his poem "Canto," which appeared in the fall 2008 issue. Ray is the author of a number of books of poetry and the winner of several awards, including the 1997 PEN / Oakland Josephine Miles Book Award and the 2003 Minnesota Book Award for Poetry.

The fifty poems published in the fall 2008 and spring 2009 issues of FWJ, excluding the work of the featured poet in each issue, were considered by Professor Anna Leahy, who admitted the task of selecting a winner was both fun and difficult. Here is how she made her decision:

I have chosen "Canto" by Ray Gonzalez for special recognition with the Editor's Prize in Poetry, but I also would like to note "Interior with a Violin" by **Rebecca B. Rank** and "Saint Monica Takes Communion Twice" by **Mary Biddinger** as honorable mentions.

I'm surprised that I was enamored with two prose poems, but I found that all three of these poems use language in lively, unexpected, lovely ways that made me want to listen intently. The prose poem "Canto" is not prose per se and reminded me that Stanley Plumly calls such a thing a paragraph poem. The form of "Canto" is the paragraph — Gonzalez has made a formal choice, just as another poet might have used iambic pentameter. Sometimes, the paragraph as a form can make a poet lazy, distract him from attention to sound and syntax toward something too narratively linear. Gonzalez uses the form exceptionally well in "Canto," so that the reader dances and ponders through the sentences as the pacing shifts. "Canto" is a bold and sweeping poem, grounded by its detail and brevity.

Biddinger's paragraph poem is quite different, but also uses the form well to achieve a rush of juxtaposition and a distinct voice. Rank's poem has somewhat the opposite feel as Biddinger's, with plenty of enjambed lines, spacing between lines, and a voice that is both halting and urgently pushing on. These two poems deserve recognition in part because they demonstrate the range that *Fifth Wednesday Journal* encompasses.

—

Anna Leahy is professor of English and Creative Writing at Chapman University in Orange, California. Her book, *Constituents of Matter*, won the Wick Poetry Prize and was published by Kent State University Press (2007).

FICTION

Our choices for fiction are **Andrew Coburn** for "Hearty Women," which appeared in the spring 2009 issue, and **Diana Joyce** for "Légispota,"which appeared in fall 2008. Andrew is the author of numerous short stories and thirteen novels; Diana has a B.A. in German Studies and Psychology from the University of Pennsylvania and a certificate in creative writing from the University of Chicago. She is an M.F.A. candidate at Northwestern University.

The editors selected five stories from the twenty-three published in the fall 2008 and spring 2009 issues of FWJ and asked Professor Keith Gandal to tell us which should receive the Editor's Prize. After several weeks and as many times through the stories, this is how he made his decision:

"Hearty Women": This story hits all the cylinders. It is a pleasure to read: Line by line and page after page, the reader is engaged, delighted, and rewarded with carefully crafted phrases and wit. In addition, the story has an easy narrative drive; the reader feels taken somewhere. And by the end, the reader has been treated, in a mere twenty pages, to a concise tale of impressive scope and depth: We follow nearly the entire adult lives of our two female protagonists as they experience marriage, friendship, (creative) work, and various American eras and administrations; other people come into it, and we get to know them as well. Their lives are at once interesting and commonplace or familiar (readers can feel their own lives here): unexpected things happen; love fails to develop where it is expected, and it movingly appears where not expected (in a marriage made not for love); one of the main characters has an affair with a married man but it ends in a very unexpected manner; a chronically sick spouse surprisingly heals, and the previously healthy spouse suddenly declines; nobody experiences fame or tremendous success, but they keep working and creating and remain intelligent. In the end, female friendships among three "hearty women" resuscitate or survive, but the story never feels heavy-handed or ideological. The story has an imaginative virtuosity (indeed, it is written by a male author) and a mature sense of realism.

"Légiposta" likewise has an impressive scope; the reader experiences the protagonist as both a mature man in America and as a youth in Hungary. The seeming return of a dazzling female acquaintance from the faraway past who had a singular and important effect on the man's spirit and indeed his life trajectory is in itself a fascinating theme, and the author (here a woman writing a male protagonist) draws us in carefully, as we move from present-day New York to Budapest in 1956, with the Russian tanks moving in, and back. We are engaged with the man's life story (and the particular rhythms of his speech and his amusing verbal "mistakes" remind us he is an immigrant), a story that breathes life into the historical events about which the reader probably knows only the bare historical facts: And this too is a pleasure for the reader. History takes on three dimensions, but it inflates smoothly because we are also aware that this is all a flashback in preparation for a surprise reunion, seemingly with this long-ago female acquaintance. But the story has one major, final surprise to throw at the reader, and a couple of minor ones. We don't see where the story is going, and suddenly it has taken us to a place neither the protagonist nor the reader saw coming. Both comic and sad, this is a successfully realistic story about, among other things, the painful and inevitable losses involved in growing older.

Keith Gandal is professor of English at Northern Illinois University. He is the author of a novel, *Cleveland Anonymous*. He is also the author of *The Gun and the Pen: Hemingway, Fitzgerald, Faulkner and the Fiction of Mobilization* (Oxford UP, 2008); *The Virtues of the Vicious: Jacob Riis, Stephen Crane and the Spectacle of the Slum* (Oxford, 1997) and *Class Representation in Modern Fiction and Film* (Palgrave Macmillan, 2007).

PHOTOGRAPHY

Our choice for the Editor's Prize for photography is **Harry Wilson** for "Classroom, Turkey," which was published in the fall 2008 issue. Wilson is a retired professor of art at Bakersfield College and his photos have been exhibited widely.

The editors selected five photos from the thirty published in the fall 2008 and spring 2009 issues of FWJ and asked Professor Barbara DeGenevieve to tell us which should receive the Editor's Prize. This is how she made her decision:

Making a choice between images that are made by photographers who all have reached a certain level of accomplishment is difficult. To first narrow the group to five was the easy part. To make the finer distinctions was the hard part. At this point, the choice is never simply based on "quality" of image or vision. Any judgment about art always contains a bias and has more to do with the taste or aesthetic of the viewer/judge than any agreed upon standard of excellence.

That being said, there has to be something in the image that draws me to it and sets off a thought process that goes far beyond the image's denotative content. I am most drawn to images that unsettle me and leave me with questions about how and why the world comes to be as it is — visually, culturally, psychologically, politically. The image "Classroom, Turkey" fulfilled my personal requirements for intellectual engagement more than any other. The circumstances of this particular school environment, the ambiguity of the child's gender, the high POV of the camera, all conspire to question the cultural politics of education and the acquisition of knowledge.

As honorable mention, I'd also like to acknowledge **Leigh Wells** for "Palm Beach, Coney Island" and "Transamerican Picnic," both of which appeared in the spring 2009 issue. Not as heavily laden with social commentary, "Palm Beach, Coney Island" and "Transamerican Picnic" evoke atmospheres that are both beautiful and threatening. The choice to shoot at night creates an intriguingly "humanless" portrait of two locations that would never be seen as they have been photographed.

All three of these images are compelling and deserve recognition.

Barbara DeGenevieve is an interdisciplinary artist who works in photography, video, and performance. She received her M.F.A. in photography from the University of New Mexico and teaches at the School of the Art Institute of Chicago where she is a professor and Chairperson of the Photography Department.

ON MAKING A POEM: AN INTERVIEW WITH MICHAEL VAN WALLEGHEN

By James Ballowe
July 2009

FWJ: *Those of us who have followed your work will recognize in the four poems that appear here a syntax and themes that have been evolving in the six books you have published since 1975: a poetic line that relentlessly pursues, then captures and illuminates briefly a truth that confronts both the poet and the reader. I think you define how this works in lines from "Once More With Mother on the Beach," a poem that appeared in* **In the Black Window** *in 2003. The narrator of that poem, looking through binoculars, explains to his mother, bothered by cataracts, that the female seagull she believes is limping is, in fact, fine: "healthy / in her zoom-close proximity / to the point of corpulence / almost, / and in glad possession / of a large, / dead fish — / a narrative turn / at once / so dissonant, / so thoroughly / familiar, / it makes us stop / and laugh out loud / before we start again / on living wills, / my brother's / suicide, / and why it is / I see her / only once a year..." What is the word for this? Juxtaposition?*

MVW: I don't know if the word for what you intuit as a structural device is something as discreet as "juxtaposition." I certainly have no conscious awareness of placing one contradiction or opposition against another in any deliberate way. I'm pretty certain that I have no preordained thematic intentions in this regard. I work pretty much in the dark; so when you say that I have "a poetic line that relentlessly pursues ... and illuminates briefly a truth..." I can only say that I pursue a narrative line that makes sense, or seems true, in terms of my lived experience. In other words, I'm just rather desperately trying to construct a coherent, interesting narrative. If it works, I'm astonished. I don't know how I did it. It's a goddamn miracle — a discovery, that partakes, I suppose of the epiphanic. I would hope the reader feels somewhat the same. The poem from which you quote, by the way, is written in broken, staggered lines — so in a line that breaks in the middle, drops down and continues, the middle line ending is often not as heavily end–stopped as the diagonal slash in your quotation might indicate. In other words, the line is more relaxed and perhaps more congenial to the particular narrative at hand. Mother and son having a conversation on the beach.

FWJ: *These four poems in FWJ take place in geographies you know intimately. Michigan where you were born; Kentucky, through* which you have passed. "*Barefoot on the Sandy Path of My Second Childhood*" *takes place in Florida, where your parents lived after your father's retirement. But these familiar places harbor unsettling experiences where past and present are confused by startling discoveries and images. These new poems, naturally enough, offer a perspective on life that comes after, as you say, "one's first pubescent / year of ... retirement." Is this time, then, for the invention of a narrative to explain one's life? Is it time for metamorphosing into creatures we never were?*

MVW: Well, I think it's a universal tendency, after a certain age, to conflate past and present. What happened long ago keeps coming back rather more vividly than it did when you were younger. And yes, I think for me at least, it does become time "for the invention of a narrative to explain one's life." For me, the key word here would be "invention." A narrative that purports to stay true to the literal facts of one's life would seem to provide little by way of explanatory insight, unless those facts were meditated upon and given some metaphorical value. Why not invent a parallel universe of sorts where what happens may be patently absurd in terms of real world experience or expectations, but may indeed be metaphorically true and incisive in ways that a literal narrative could never be — also funnier and more interesting perhaps? I look back on my childhood sometimes with puzzled disbelief. Were things really so weird and unlikely as all of that? Well, yes — and as I think about those events from this perspective in time, that quality of strangeness can only be invented.

FWJ: *In* **The Last Neanderthal***, 1999, you have two poems with titles that would seem to many readers to define the art of poetry: "Clarity" and "Beauty." You end the first by writing of your memory of the "leopard frog / beside a tiny, coal-black bullhead, / ...having achieved, in the mind's eye / the perfect clarity of last things." And in "Beauty" you write of finding in the act of having created the phrase "sunwashed seabirds" that "I knew there was something, born / perhaps of the heart's pure yearning / that would save my life: Beauty / the name for those birds was Beauty." The epigraph to this poem is from Paul Valéry's* **The Art of Poetry***: "There is nothing so beautiful as that which does not exist." Is this what has caused you to write for all these years?*

MVW: Let me first say something about clarity, not the poem necessarily, but the poetic value of the thing itself. I prize it rather highly. I like sharp, clear images and a syntax that is crisp and readily understood. The metaphorical implications of any given poem are another matter altogether. These may be very complicated and resonant indeed — so it's not simplicity that I aspire to — but *clarity* itself is very attractive. I like Louise Gluck for her clarity, for instance, but I understand her to be pretty daunting at times and often I feel I don't "understand" her very well at all, if by that we mean the ability to come away with something that might be paraphrased as *meaning* one thing or another. I love her clarity, however. Her syntax. Her dramatic instinct. Her tone. I'm perfectly happy to live with her "difficulty" forever. So, yes, clarity is very much a part of my poetic ambition.

Beauty, also, is something I believe in, but as the quotation suggests, as a spiritual ideal. We can argue about what is beautiful, but I believe it's less a real quality than a "yearning." In other words, it is a transcendent value. Should you look up the Valery quote, it comes as almost a footnote at the end of the book. I took it to heart.

FWJ: *Your poetry contains story lines anchored in geologic and natural history, religion, and memory of family and of your own experiences. What do you think is the poet's principal duty to the reader? To tell a compelling story? To be philosophical? Something other?*

MVW: I'll settle for being interesting. Who wants to be philosophical? I love E.A. Robinson, for example, but not in his philosophical mode. Try teaching "The Man Against the Sky" sometime. As for allusions to science, religion, or anything else out there in the world of ideas, why not? Use everything you can, that's my motto. I just don't know very much, or I'd stretch further. I always used to tell students to use whatever vocabularies they were most comfortable with. If you're a physics major or have an interest in that area, why deprive yourself? As for memory of family and personal experience, how could one do without it? — unless maybe you were a Language Poet. I marvel at people who find that kind of writing interesting. But after a certain age, I feel no obligation in that direction.

FWJ: *Your poetry has been described as free verse. Yet, it is as tightly controlled as the poetry of Yeats. Does the phrase "free verse" describe what you do?*

MVW: I would just say that I write a very formal kind of free verse. I'm certainly not writing in syllabics, meter, or rhyme — but if you were to count stresses within any given line, two or three of them would be the norm. So that's a formality of sorts — and a lot of it has to do with how I use my eye. While I'm perfectly comfortable with lines of uneven length in other poets, I find that keeping my lines as uniformly short as they are becomes a way of putting pressure on the language, in the same way perhaps that meter and other devices do in traditionally "formal" poems. I know it makes me sound compulsive, but that's the kind of guy I am.

FWJ: *Are these four poems a promise of another book?*

MVW: Yes, another book is on the way, and these four poems will be included. I've been doing a lot of rewriting lately and throwing away poems that I thought would be part of the final manuscript but now don't seem to fit. I've never done that before to this extent. But now I seem to have all the time in the world. In any event, I should have another book out by the end of next year. I think I'm going to call it: *Life On Other Planets*. It sounds perfectly descriptive of where I find myself to be at present.

———

James Ballowe is a poet and essayist. He is also Distinguished Professor of English Emeritus at Bradley University. His latest book is *A Man of Salt and Trees: The Life of Joy Morton* (Northern Illinois University Press, 2009), a biography of the founder of Morton Salt and The Morton Arboretum.

THE GOLGOTHA FUN PARK
Michael Van Walleghen

There's a sign that tells you
THIS IS IT,
                but the truth is

it's been boarded up for years
and so thickly overgrown
with brambly hawthorn now

you could drive right past it
and never guess a thing ...

As a matter of fact,
once full spring arrives
in this part of rural Kentucky,

you probably couldn't see it
from a balloon.
               You'd almost
have to be stopped for a flat tire

not more than three feet away
from the old driveway marker
before you saw the wire gate —

and desperate beyond all fear
of being shot
               or torn apart
by dogs
          to ignore the signs
forbidding trespass there ...

On the other hand,
              although
I'd brought along
            a pint of gin

I didn't have a lug wrench
or a working cell phone either ...

So maybe there was a house
at the end of this driveway —
a guy who could fix things …

which line
            of nimble reasoning
had me stumbling up a hill
of glass
            and broken concrete

— through sapling thickets
creeper vines
            and thorn bush —

in practically no time
                        at all

until I found myself
bleeding through my shirt
and staring eye to eye

with Jesus Christ himself.

He stood about eight feet tall
and was roughly cast
in gray cement
            that had once

been painted blue —
                        the way
a child might color him
in Sunday school.
                        He was also

tilted
            by about twenty degrees
like frost-heaved
                        graveyard sculpture
            .

and kept from falling over
by a convenient piece
of railing
            from a blown-down
swan
            and horseless carousel …

Part Octopus
                    part Ferris Wheel
part house trailer
                    corn dog
and bible tent …
                    It's hard to believe

this whole dead universe
                         of dizzy
fun park junk,
                    lying disarticulate
and rusting now
                    all around him
in the weeds,
                    was heaven once

where every weekend
all through summer
                         he suffered
the little children
                    to come unto him
and forbade them not …

for such,
                    as we all know
was the real
                    and everlasting
Kingdom of Heaven —

which would seem to have been
firmly located
                    just inside
the cosmic
                    skull of God

until
        the Big Bang of course —
which together
                    with integration
evolution
                    and homosexuals

ruined everything:
                    childhood
the Golgotha Fun Park …

and whatever else
                    we could think
to talk about
                    for twenty long miles

in that slow
                    Pentecostal
police car
                    that kindly stopped
and drove me back
                    still bleeding
to my Holiday Inn motel.

THE RETURN
Michael Van Walleghen

A Siberian tiger leaps the moat
and granite cliff of his enclosure

then scrambles to his dizzy feet
thirty thousand years from now —

or perhaps some equal distance
back there in his Ice Age past

where, alas, it still smells human
but not so human as it did

this afternoon, before the day's
last grade school field trip

wandered vaguely off one by one
like a nursing home excursion

disremembering their foggy bus —
the litter of their peanut shells

and paper cups inauspiciously
still afloat at dusk as autumn

leaves upon his black lagoon …
or garbage in a stopped up sink.

Then, one by one, the stars
come out, the moon rises

and suddenly as an ambulance
alarm, a spooked out elephant

or a spear struck mammoth
starts trumpeting somewhere

back behind the monkey house …
until the whole zoo comes awake

and he finds himself staring
into the red revolving lights

of a rhinoceros sized police car
while all around him the moon

— white eyes of circling hyenas
or zoo attendants with flashlights

start closing in. If he were human
they'd probably be after him again

for peeing in the cafeteria sink
and wandering off into the dark

two o'clock, Siberian morning
in nothing but his underwear.

But as it happens, he's a tiger now
and at the moment, neither here

nor there, unless they shoot him.
Unless he kills somebody. Unless

he can remember, in another life
throwing peanuts to the polar bears

at the Belle Isle Zoo — six years old.
His father right there beside him.

THE FROZEN BOY
Michael Van Walleghen

Unlike most recent sea level
discoveries, our expedition
found this specimen frozen

and complete, dead center
of the Michigan Glacier …

a wasteland we all know
from eons of exploration
to be heavily crevassed,

two and a half miles thick,
and swept by winds approaching

three hundred miles an hour —
making its whole vast surface
inimical to even bacterial life

and more or less unreachable
by anything but nuclear sled.

And yet this particular cadaver
would seem to have gotten here
wearing ice skates. *Ice skates?*

No one knew what they were.
We had to run a search …

It seems the kind he had on
were "ON SALE," (whatever
that means) back in the age

of streetcars and cement,
ten thousand years ago. So …

at this point, the only theory
that makes any sense at all
is that he somehow fell

from a primitive "airship,"
although we freely admit

that even if such contraptions
did in fact exist, our theory
still stumbles rather clumsily

over those anomalous skates —
but here is where we are so far:

An airship, maybe the last
one to "fly" after the earth
has switched magnetic poles,

suddenly loses its bearings
high over the Michigan Glacier,

then turns straight into the path
of a furious glacial tornado —
whereupon the captain orders

all hands to lace up their skates
and standby to parachute

into the winds of certain death …
So far, so good. Except we can't
find any parachutes, other bodies,

or any wreckage whatsoever …
But we've just chipped loose

an odd scrap of yellow paper
from his thin blue mitten
with the word "TRANSFER"

in bold letters, written on it —
followed by "Jefferson Ave.,"

then some other writing I can't
make out. The word "transfer"
however, in pre-Ice Age English

means to move something
from one place to another …

In which case, can we suppose
this boy was "transferred" here
by some superior intelligence

from another planet? Why not?
Then the cryptic "Jefferson Ave."

could be their cosmic address
and he could be a boy riding
on a Jefferson streetcar there

in his ice skates. His shoes lost
or stolen, his corduroy pants
filling up with black despair …

and after that, a brief wobbly
walk on his home cement —

before he somehow ends up
here, on the Michigan Glacier

where we can study him
and so invent some narrative
that might explain his life.

BAREFOOT ON THE SANDY PATH
OF MY SECOND CHILDHOOD
Michael Van Walleghen

My second childhood
the one I'm living now

resembles almost nothing
I remember from the first …

In this one, for instance
my parents are almost

non-existent, my brother
too — their restless shades

and idle ashes all dispersed
— dispersed at last —

in this first, pubescent
year of my retirement,

into wind-changing light
and the ambient air …

I wear my baseball hat
backwards now. I've even

quit wearing shoes …
And yea, though I run

leaping and barefoot
day after day, down

the steep, sandy path
of the rest of my life

I'm not insane. Half
a broken beer bottle

could change things
in a hurry. Besides glass

of course, I watch out
for disposable diapers,

fishhooks, nails … I eat
a good breakfast too,

watch my blood pressure,
and wrap the arthritic

left knee of encroaching
old age with the humble

zeal of an Albanian nun —
before taking off again

like a wobbly biplane
down the Kitty Hawk hill

of a two-week vacation …
which, by some accident

of gravity divided by time,
ends with a belly flop

into the same still waters
as the day before yesterday

where I've just learned
how to swim. Otherwise

my parents are playing
pinochle on the porch —

the early mosquitoes
trumping them blind …

then making me come in
all shivering and blue

as my unborn brother,
after a grand mal seizure

face down in the lake
four years later. And later,

before he caught breath
swimming up from the dead

on our wet kitchen floor —
I memorized the sinister

hiss of our Coleman lamp
and that two-note song

the frogs were singing …
who wanted him back —

floating frog-belly white
in the dissonant reeds

of my emeritus sleep
on that Stygian shore.

"Oh, stop it," she had said, coldly. Adding, "God, it's tiresome. Everything's not *always* your fault."

What was he to make of that? Uneasiness gathered in his chest, as he entered the park. He walked quickly; it surprised him how many people were out this early. In the past, years earlier, he had come to the park on a Saturday morning to ride his bike as early as this, and there had not been so many people, he was quite certain of that. The air was warm already; it could have been midday, but he always liked the heat. And this was good — to be out and about, to be moving.

When he climbed the stairs to the reservoir, he saw how the forsythia bushes were beginning to sprinkle their yellow across the wall, and he thought how she would comment on that, if she were with him, and not back home in bed, angry. He passed by a middle-aged couple holding hands, and felt his uneasiness return, and also he was ashamed. She said things were not always his fault, but it seemed to him they often were. He could not run the office effectively. He could not get it all done. This is what made him ashamed. She had called him a workaholic, and the word puzzled him — as though someone had told him he had diabetes when he'd never once tested with high sugars. Perhaps he should have said, No, I *have* to stay that late, I can't get all the work done. Perhaps he should have said, It *scares* me that I can't get everything done. But he did not believe, in spite of all that was said and done these days — he did not believe women meant it when they said they wanted to see vulnerability in men. So he had explained once more, what it was to stay in practice alone these days. By the time the patients leave, he had said, I have all those charts, and there are calls to make — but oh, the memory of his own voice, tense and quiet, made him terribly uneasy. He did not want to fail at this.

He thought again of her cold voice, "Not *every*thing is always your fault." He could not remember what had come before, to what — specifically — she was responding. But it was an accusation that caused a deep ache within him to stir, to start its slow climb up his heart. It's true that he had felt that his father's rages at his mother were his fault; as a small child he had been afraid to go to school, afraid his mother would be hurt. Children believe everything is their fault; this he knew. But the sense of responsibility had weighed heavily on him, had never left him; every patient he had seen over all these years — they *were* his responsibility. He walked more quickly, suddenly remembering Agnes Manetti; he had worked for weeks to save her when she was in the ICU; years ago, it was, but he could still remember, the kidneys failing, the shutting down of the system, and he had worked one thing and then another, and she had come round, and when she finally opened her eyes and realized she was alive, she stared at him and said, "Goddamn you! I was ready to die! I saw a white light and felt peaceful, so *peaceful!*" And she had started to cry.

She never forgave him, Agnes Manetti.

He walked more quickly, sweat breaking on his upper lip, his brow. He would go around the reservoir three times, and when he got home —

"On your left!" came a shout, and before he could think he had stepped the wrong way, collided with a young woman runner who swore at him.

"Oh, sorry," he said. The sun came through an opening in the trees and blinded him. He could not think which way to go.

YOU ARE WHAT YOU OWE
Ira Wood

Nonfiction

Now I had proof. I was not paranoid. Here it was, exposed in black and white, what every writer knew deep down but didn't dare to think.

The article, in the newsletter of the National Writers Union, reported on an agent following up on a manuscript he'd sent an editor. The editor said that he liked the book well enough but asked, "What's the author like?"

"She's blonde, she's thirty years old, and she's adorable," the agent said, and the editor made an offer for the book.

Even famous writers, no matter how many books they've written or great reviews they've received, secretly feel like starter wives, fearful of being replaced in their publisher's eyes by the next big talent, the new young thing. When I was thirty-five, my own first novel was published to wonderful attention. My publisher was ecstatic. "You're hot!" But not for long. Like the freshman girl who did it under the bleachers with the captain of the football team, I couldn't even get him to return my calls.

Sooner or later, every writer I know decides he can do a better job than his publisher. I have a friend who was one of America's best selling authors, an Oprah Book Club choice. But when his books started selling thousands of copies instead of hundreds of thousands, he concluded his publisher was at fault. Reading a few how-to books written by former publishing industry publicists, he hired his own former publishing industry publicist to devise a marketing plan that his publishers might have come up with had they not been preoccupied by the new young thing on their list whose work was more "commercial" — a category of books that is anathema to serious writers unless it describes their own.

I too thought I could do it better than my publisher. This is largely why I became a publisher. I had a business plan and a mission statement and above all the determination to treat writers with respect. I prepared for two years, telling everyone I knew that I could do it better than my publisher, reading every book I could find by former publishing industry publicists, interviewing publishers large and small, those who worked out of swank Manhattan offices and those who used an old barn as a warehouse; some who had entered the business with a strong literary vision and others who simply published books they liked. The New York publishers were cynical about the future of the book business. They trotted out the usual suspects, the chains, the media conglomerates, the Internet, and fondly reminisced about the years of six-figure advances and three-hour lunches. I asked one legendary editor how he saw himself in the changing milieu. "Once," he said, "I felt like I was playing center field for the Yankees and now I'm Dilbert." But I pressed on, pigeonholing anyone who had something to teach me and ten minutes to spare, searching for my own quiet corner of the book world and finding it in the midst of all-out madness.

Book Expo America is a bloated media carnival of high-tech booths and hyperbolic lit buzz, the largest book trade show in the world, the NASCAR of *belles-lettres*, a writhing monkey barrel of marketing professionals climbing over each other for attention. Indoor skyscrapers of polyurethane tubing frame pavilions as long as football fields with turf of plush red carpet. Backlit blow-ups of book jackets and writers with palsied smiles line the aisles like posters in a freak show midway. Librarians, booksellers, critics, authors, bloggers, and bobbing throngs of bookbiz junketeers push folding carts full of posters, baseball caps, tote bags, beach balls, ballpoints, T-shirts, mouse pads, and every manner of promo crap ever shipped out of the People's Republic of China. Bill Clinton signs books for a line of fans a quarter mile long. Richard Simmons in purple velvet running shorts does jumping jacks in the aisle. Strippers in pink satin garter belts hawk a celebrity madam tell-all in a mock nineteenth-century brothel erected next to a fifty-foot-high Lego display. Three-hundred-pound Dixieland musicians wearing Hawaiian leis play the "Muskrat Ramble" while an Elvis imitator fumbles with the crotch of his rhinestone jumpsuit and poses for a snapshot with the assistant manager of a Barnes & Noble from Erie, Pennsylvania.

But far from the stacks of advance reading copies doled out by young publicity assistants in tight, pinstripe pantsuits, beyond the sleek, gray-carpeted booths of the academic presses and the garish hawkers of bookstore novelties, through the double doors of the satellite convention hall, to the right of the restrooms and the left of the five-dollar-pretzel vendor, are the aisles of the independent publishers. Foot traffic is slower here, the lighting subdued, the freebies modest, the visitors cautious. They are offering penny candy here, postcards, bookmarks, bound galleys with titles promising sex and revolution. Their covers show full frontal nudes, brown-skinned peoples carrying rifles, a gallant head shot of a young Noam Chomsky. A librarian from Little Rock making her way from the ladies' room peers warily up the aisle. The owner of an Annie's Book Swap in western Massachusetts who spent all morning filling his cart with give-away books to sell back at the store, furtively grabs a copy of *Going Down: Perfecting the Art of a Good Blowjob.*

While the New York publishers wore suits from Barney's and Prada loafers, this was a dress-down world of turtlenecks and sneakers, peasant skirts and motorcycle boots, prideful independents who sneered at the conglomerate giants. Literature was paramount; money beside the point. I had finally found my people. Or so I imagined.

Obscured by my romantic delusions was the fact that while the most cynical of these crusading independents were indeed strapped for cash, others were backed by an invisible fortune. The frumpy ex-hippie in granny glasses was financed by a cosmetics heiress who pumped seed money into the presses that published her books. The overfed wunderkind dressed head to toe in black denim was the son of a world famous fashionista. A psychiatrist who left his practice after amassing a huge portfolio; the scion of a Brazillian industrial fortune (whom I had thought hearing impaired until I understood he had so much money there was nothing he needed pay attention to); a fundraising savant who played the foundations like a pinball wizard; the third son of the 14th Earl of Cricklade, simply had more to fall back on than book sales. I summoned the courage to ask the advice of an infamous counterculture publisher whose company had survived for decades and introduced some of America's best known authors — all of whom had gone on to publish with New York presses after making it big. A hulking bear of a man who wore an old, flannel shirt and a leather sheath with a long hunting knife, he dropped a thick calloused hand on my shoulder and said, "Friend, you are what you owe."

Having been inculcated by my forebears with a fear of debt in any form, mortgages, bank loans, car payments — when my grandfather took his extended family out once a year to Ratner's, a dairy restaurant on the Lower East Side of Manhattan, he insisted on paying the bill *before* we ate — I continued my research with less enthusiasm. But by now my wife, Marge, had grown exasperated and committed us to a point of no return, writing a letter to twenty-five, well-known writer-friends asking them to recommend manuscripts. Once the post office box began to fill there was no turning back.

I was obsessed with appearing legitimate. Who was I to claim to be a publisher? Why would critics review our books? Why would bookstores carry them? Did it matter that the title page of our books located us in a tiny Massachusetts fishing village rather than a big city? What would happen if agents found out our office was a one-room winter rental with no heat? I invented an editorial staff and put their bios on the website, hip young Ivy League grads in their twenties with cool names. Elvis Kahn was my favorite. He rose from the ranks of editorial assistant to acquisitions editor and was the point man for many negotiations, an amusing situation until I was introduced to a book page editor with whom I had been talking via telephone, as Elvis, for over a year. But first and foremost was the mission to support writers.

When we first started Leapfrog, we were so dedicated that we would read every submission that arrived — sometimes all the way through! — and write two-page letters full of editing suggestions. Soon word got out: Leapfrog Press was the best place in the country to get rejected. Even if they don't publish your book, they critique it! The slush pile grew to the height of a refrigerator and, if you caught sight of it in just the wrong light, it seemed to have eyes and fangs and sneer at you like the Thurber cartoon of a house morphed into an angry woman's face. It took me years to get Marge to stop reading every page of every book in the slush pile. I learned my own lesson after throwing a manuscript across the room.

It was late, I was tired, glossing over it in that kind of numb state in which you follow the credits of a movie when I realized it was not an erotic novel I was holding in my hands, but puerile, fetishistic, pornography about red welts on bare buttocks and little girls' panties and pee, the infantile fantasy of an stunted, child-man's mind. Nor did I pick up the pages but swept them into a plastic garbage bag. As the address on the return envelope was from a nearby town, and I imagined being stalked for a reply, I scribbled, "Sorry, we don't publish this sort of thing," taped it closed in lieu of licking it and washed my hands. Some days later I received an e-mail reply from the writer, "Thank you, Ira, for being so nice."

Having been a writer before I was a publisher doomed me to be nice, like a former waiter compelled to over tip. Only once in ten years do I remember losing it, doing something blatantly nasty to a writer we published. Here was a guy whose career we had saved, who, if not dead in the water when he approached us, had a lot of trouble placing his work.

He had had one groundbreaking book which won a major prize and many afterwards which sold in diminishing numbers. But he was a tireless self promoter. He blogged, he hosted a reading series, he collected favors, he schmoozed. He submitted a novel that was almost published by a prestigious New York press, almost, but was missing something that no editor was able to pinpoint. If little Leapfrog, stranded on outermost Cape Cod, having upgraded its corporate headquarters to a grain warehouse with no windows, had proved itself adept at anything it was the resurrection of near misses: diagnosing the need for a new beginning, a tighter plot, a selling title; a publicity hook or simply an understanding of the mood of the country. (One of our most successful titles, a West Coast best-seller, was rejected in New York during the early Bush years because no editor there could imagine that a hilarious satire about a gay Jewish liberal trapped in a fundamentalist bible college could find a market.) The book by the self-promoter enjoyed respectable advance sales. The author and I spent a year together on editing and promotion; we were texting every day.

OUTBOX: LAT revu sched for 12/1.

INBOX: ^5! U d'man!

But after a while, we began to spat like rock musicians cooped up together on a thirty-city tour or, more accurately, a married couple, each of whom feels their work is invisible to the other.

INBOX: ??? Did U call Union SQ B&N to gt me rdg there?

OUTBOX: Only 300 times.

Expectations are high in publishing. It's difficult for an author to understand why he wasn't reviewed in *The New York Times*, or why his recent books fizzle when his first did well. Or why a book about an unrepentant shopaholic or an untrainable dog gets a lot of attention while an insightful, family character study is all but neglected. A writer can blame himself, of course, but what did he do except sacrifice four years of his life to hard work and research? Sooner or later most writers start to think they can do a better job than their publisher.

When I started to receive daily e-mails demanding that I re-submit his book to critics who had declined to review it, when he accused me of spending more time and money on another author's book, I sent him a rotten *Kirkus*.

Kirkus is one of the most esteemed of the advance trade reviews, those magazines that critique books two to three months before they are made available for sale. A really good *Kirkus* can generate a rush of calls from movie producers; a bad one means surprisingly little. Except to an author. A bad *Kirkus*, with its razor-sharp invective, can signal the arrival of Armageddon to an author who has been waiting years for the public's response. Most publishers are disappointed by an unfavorable *Kirkus* and simply file it away. But I figured a little humility was in order here, and I duly faxed it on. Our relations were noticeably more cordial after that and have been ever since.

Although publishers large and small delegate their slush piles to the lowliest dogsbodies in the organization, they're usually too superstitious to disregard them entirely and do read them, however slowly and partially, because they always have the nagging fear that they might be rejecting a work of genius. *War and Peace, Remembrance of Things Past, To Kill a Mockingbird*, were all rejected by publishers. Some nitwit even passed on the *Joy of Cooking*. We found one of our most successful books through the slush pile. It was brilliant, original and topical and scholarly; Marge had selected it out of hundreds of manuscripts and kept hounding me to read it. Once I did, I called the author immediately but by that time he was dead. We had missed him by three weeks. We couldn't tell the widow we weren't going to publish her husband's magnum opus, but we weren't real keen on the book's chances. We had nobody to send on tour, nobody to do interviews, no future young talent for the media to discover. In despair, I turned to the publicist of one of the country's most successful literary publishers. "Oh, Ira, don't be discouraged," she said. "Dead authors can be great to work with." Better, sad to say, than some live ones.

While the dead author's book caught a huge break, hailed by the press as the second coming of *A Confederacy of Dunces* — the posthumous comic novel that won its author a Pulitzer Prize — I encountered a number of authors who promised to help promote their titles but, once the book was accepted, had no intention of following through.

It's disheartening when a writer turns out to have stage fright and gives a terrible performance. We published a photogenic young woman who looked like sex itself in a black, leather mini-skirt but who mumbled through her first chapter at a bookstore appearance as if listing a prescription drug's side effects on a radio commercial. There's no way of telling who can perform and who cannot. I conversed for a year via telephone with an articulate novelist whom we arranged to have read at a book festival. I knew him only from his publicity head shot and didn't recognize him at the airport. Far from the dashing outdoorsman with a tweed hat and a lecherous twinkle in his eye, he stumbled into the baggage claim area like an elderly Walt Whitman and, in fact, read like Whitman himself, recorded in 1890 on an Edison wax cylinder. An author doesn't have to be a great performer. She can develop a fan base in a newspaper column, a cable TV chat show. But some authors, many of whom are academics, view a new book as a bullet point in their resume and their publisher as something like the department secretary.

My least favorite author — the one who was less helpful than the dead one, and here I am going to take pains to conceal his identity, so let's call him Errol Schmuck — not only refused to make author appearances without being paid, but to proofread his book. "Man, I'm a poet, I'm not into this proofreading jive and besides, I've got finals to grade." Proofreading your manuscript, as every writer knows, is an important thing to do, perhaps especially so for poetry. Poets use so few words to say so much that each word carries more weight than that of a work of prose. Only the poet knows the precise rhythm and punctuation and break in the line; no copy editor can verify what is intended. So a poet, of all writers, needs to be the one to make the final judgment on the manuscript. But Errol Schmuck had finals to grade and did not catch the elimination of a page break which resulted in the fusing of two poems.

The reviews, I'm happy to say, were splendid. Apparently, nobody noticed. Except Errol Schmuck, who demanded a nationwide recall. We placed an errata sheet in the small first printing, offered to exchange all misprinted copies for a new one, and immediately ran a corrected second printing. End of story.

Not quite. The first telephone call came at midnight. Although I wasn't in the office to answer, I was able to savor it and all those that followed on the answering machine, counting the many ways you can call someone a cheap Jew without actually saying it. I sort of enjoyed the subsequent series of blistering e-mails we exchanged but not the calls from booksellers who wanted to know what to do about the broad-shouldered, very angry man who planted himself at the check-out counter with an armful of books from their shelves, claiming that he was the author, that the books were "tainted" and that he demanded they be returned to the publisher. Yes, of course, we accepted them. I then paid the distributor to comb through every last book in the warehouse. For years the notice on our website read: "You may be in possession of a book with a serious error. This is a rare book and may be of considerable value to collectors. We will gladly exchange it for a corrected copy from a subsequent printing." We never had a taker; not one.

Before I began Leapfrog Press I imagined publishers who wore wide wale corduroys and French blue shirts with flamboyant bow ties, who worked late into the night blue-penciling manuscripts then went for martinis with starry-eyed young women editors to whom they were legends. I didn't own a blue pencil, but I did wear corduroys and a sweater and a muffler, and I did work late into the night reading manuscripts next to the space heater in my office, willing them to captivate me with the same plaintive longing with which I stared into the refrigerator at lunch time, as if simply looking long and hard enough would give rise to something I could actually eat, or in this case, sell.

Why, I wondered, had I ever wanted to sell books instead of write them? It wasn't that people didn't love books and want to read them, they just didn't see why they should buy them retail. And why would they when books were free in libraries and selling for pennies online? Sometimes, as the wind battered the building and the clocked ticked to daybreak, as the reality of money and sales or, to be honest, the lack of both, kept me up at night, I imagined thousands of unsold books returning to our warehouse from bookstores all over America — on pallets, in boxes, on trucks, in trains, mounting in piles like the columns of debt in my monthly statements. In an effort to soothe myself to sleep I made lists, conjuring all the things that were easier to sell than books — pizza, tattoos, T-shirts. One night I imagined standing on a street corner hawking a pair of underpants. A ridiculous comparison but one that, in my increasingly addled frame of mind, deserved scrutiny. People needed underpants. Most people did not feel they *needed* a book. Nor were critics likely to write a sarcastic review of a pair of underpants. And who would ever give a pair of used underpants to a friend — "Have you worn this? I think you'll enjoy it." — or sell it to a used underwear dealer? But the most shameful thing was the way I began to view books, once a treasured source of knowledge and delight, now a symbol of failure and pain.

One day, however, I received a telephone call from a starry-eyed young woman editor to whom I was apparently a legend. Her voice was hesitant. "I'm so sorry to interrupt you but I … me and my backers, that is … are starting a small press." Recalling my own timid questions at BEA and the publishers who took the time to answer them I invited her up to my office.

"We l-o-v-e Leapfrog Press," she said upon driving two hours to get here and shyly admitted she was copying our website design, our mission statement, the "look" of our books. "Leapfrog is so cool," she said, "so cutting edge."

She picked my brain for details I had forgotten years ago, and I had to admit to an unexpected *frisson* to the attentions of a young woman who saw in me everything I had wanted to become. But surrounded by stacks of titles we had published, giant posters of book covers, boxes of promotional rubber frogs, a six-foot-long calendar board that projected the deadline of every task for the next twelve months, she found herself in paradise while I was in a prison of my own making. At one time in my life a situation such as this, a bright and energetic woman who was asking for my guidance, might have led me to fantasize one scenario while I was already beginning to conjure another. After several more meetings I was ready to make my move.

I proposed a small café this time and found a table where we would not be overheard. When she entered, late and sweetly frazzled as always, she didn't see me at first but glowed as soon as we locked eyes. When she sat down I told her I'd been thinking a lot about her. She blushed. "But," I edged closer, "there's something we need to talk about."

She looked wary.

"Promise me you'll think it over, that you won't just say no."

Now I was beginning to freak her out but, before she could answer, I came out with it: "I think you should buy Leapfrog."

"What?"

"You promised me you'd think about it."

"I did not."

"That you wouldn't just say no."

"I don't have that kind of money."

"You have backers."

"But we can't afford to buy a publishing company."

"How do you know? Do you have any idea how much you'll need

to start one? How many years it takes to develop a brand? How many books you'll have to publish before you attract a distributor? Wouldn't your backers rather take over a ten-year-old company with a great reputation than start from scratch?"

"But the financing."

"Leave the financing to me. I'll come up with something you can manage."

"I doubt that."

"Trust me. I can."

There were lawyers involved, money to raise, a contract with endless terms. We went back and forth for almost a year. Some days it seemed a deal was likely to happen; others impossible. But we persevered, pestering people for advice, looking for likely models, studying endless options — much as I done years before — she for the dream of owning a publishing company and me to get out from under one.

And once again I found myself to be a writer, an anomaly in a visually oriented world, an artist whose medium is words on paper in a century whose medium is images on screen. But having crossed the line, having spent ten years acquiring, editing, designing, and selling books, I've attained insight into the secret desires of those who publish them. Far from wanting to replace their writers with new young talent, many publishers have a more personal agenda, a longing few writers ever imagine: If I didn't have all this contractual, marketing, and publicity crap to take care of, hell, I could write a book and do it *better* than my authors.

THE END OF THE ROAD　　　　　　　　　　*Fiction*
Becky Eagleton

Her name is Misty. She does everything slowly. Not deliberately, like a house painter. Randomly. Like a cow.

My man, Spike — he's in there with Misty. I didn't figure that driving through East Texas this morning there'd be a Misty somewhere down the road. There's always a Misty at the end of some road, but I hadn't thought we were driving down it. Not yet, not this morning. And her in blue velvet in a field. But that's what happened.

At the end of this road is a field inside a high wooden fence where men in tights and capes are jousting amidst cow piles. Spike and I had straddled a bench on the edge of Ye Ole Tavern tent, drinking mead and watching the men shout insults at each other. Thrust and parry. I didn't think they were that good. The swords and long pikes looked heavy in their soft hands. The weekend warriors. The struggles at home too great for a blade.

They were so earnest, so full of the thrill. Spike was caught up in the whole thing. He'd rented the cape and the feathered hat from the costume booth and clomped around in his work boots shouting, "Wench! Wench!" That's when Misty rustled over in her blue velvet. She works the Tavern tent.

Where do these Renaissance Faire people live? What kind of house does Misty come from? Her in a boxed-in cleavage, breasts pushed over the top by whalebone, like freshly scooped ice cream stuffed into a sugar cone. Spike has a passion for sweets. For God's sake, he's the dessert cook, isn't he? At the Texarkana Country Club. "Pastry Chef," he calls himself.

The car is hot. There's no air. I've used it all up in the half hour I've been sitting out here. A guy in knickers, holding a sword, is smoking by the fence. He's seen me sitting in this car, and he's wondering why I'm in here with the windows up. I know 'cause he keeps looking over here but trying to hide it, like he's just turning his head to keep the smoke out of his eyes. But I know he's seen me. Maybe recognized me from earlier when I went up to his weapons booth and asked a lot of questions.

I'm not going to kill anybody. I *have* imagined killing someone but only in self defense. Like I'd be holding the kitchen knife up, and the attacker would slip and fall on it. But I never went further than that. Never pictured the bloody body stumbling, falling, bringing me down with it. Well, now I guess I've imagined it.

There are times when I am inexplicably sad. About once a month.

"Yeah?"

"Bunch of pansies. I could do better with a sword than any of them. They can tell that. Hell, this one ole boy's trying to get me to join his jousting team." He laughs, flexes his arms, causes the muscles to ripple and vibrate. I hate it when he does that.

"So why don't you?" I ask.

"You trying to say something?"

"No."

"'Cause if you are, just say it. Out with it, wench! Wench!" He laughs again. I look back in the car. Stupid bee's still there, hanging on the radio knob. Suddenly I'm glad it's there. Feels like company.

"Let's go home," I say. He stops jiggling. Stares at me. Reaches in his pocket and throws the car keys into the front seat. I feel my sadness evaporate and want to laugh at my silly bout of grief, fooling me again.

"Want me to drive?" I ask and wait with my hand on the door.

"Sure. I want you to drive. 'Cause I'm not leaving."

"But …"

He's turned and walking back to the entry gate, his curly hair flapping around his head like the little banners hung on the fence around the Faire. I watch his back, his casual strut, like he knows he's got a way home without me.

I feel like I'm on an island. At the gate, Spike passes a man coming out. The same man who said he'd bring me a Coke, and now he is. I want Spike to see this guy bringing me a Coke, but Spike just keeps walking and disappears behind the high wooden fence. Now I don't want this man or the damn Coke and think about getting back in the car but the bee's in there, on the steering wheel.

"Told you I'd bring you a Coke."

The guy smiles and hands me the warm bottle. I keep one hand on the open car door and one hand on the bottle.

"There's a bee in my car. So I got out." I don't want him thinking I got out just to drink a hot Coke with him.

"You scared of a bee? Hell, they won't hurt you. Unless you bother them."

I hold up the bottle. "What do I owe you?"

He lights up another cigarette. "Nothing."

"I want to pay …"

He looks back at the gate. "That your man I passed?"

"Why?"

"'Cause I think you came with him — like I say, I never forget a face." I make a decision. "Yeah, that's my man."

"Huh."

He keeps staring at the gate.

"He ain't much, you ask me."

This pisses me off, because I'm thinking the same thing. But it's mine to think and not his.

"What's it to you?" No way am I gonna drink this Coke now.

"I'm just saying." He looks straight at me. "Looks like trouble to me. That's all I'm saying."

"Well, you don't know nothin' about it." I set the bottle on top of the car.

"Huh." He throws down his cigarette. Stubs it out with his shoe. Lights another one.

"Lemme see your hands," he says.

"You can see them."

"Don't see no wedding ring."

"Don't wear it."

"Huh. Betcha don't have one."

Jesus, the balls on this guy! I slam the front car door and then the back one.

"You got a little girl?" He's looking into the backseat at my daughter's floppy doll lying on it. Cassie's at home with my Daddy. Oh, Daddy.

"What time is it?" I ask. He's surprised at my question. Good. Keep him off guard.

"Two ten."

Great. Cassie'll be at the cemetery now, playing on the old Civil War cannon while Daddy stares at Momma's grave. He drags Cassie there damn near every day at nine o'clock and two o'clock. I gotta find a better place for her to stay while I'm at work. I haven't come up with anything. Keep thinking Daddy'll slow down the cemetery visits — it's been a year.

Cassie cried yesterday when I left for work. "Don't wanna go sit Meemaw today," she whispered to me. Just a little longer baby. Please.

The guy's leaning against the car, next to me. He's got some nerve.

"Where you from?" he asks.

The cicadas are in full swing in the trees around the fence. Maybe the bee will feel their call, go visit them. The air is so still and heavy. That's when the cicadas kick in the loudest. Like they can't stand the silence. Like they know I need the accompaniment.

The guy's waiting for my answer.

"Texarkana," I say.

"Long way from here. Nice drive though." He waves his hand in front to keep the smoke from my face. "This your first Faire?"

"And my last," I say. I've got to have some of that Coke. I'm just too hot. I take the bottle from the top of the car. The guy is leaning back, looking up.

"Her name is Misty," he says.

"Whose name?" Like I don't know. The Coke is warm in my mouth, burns my nose. Maybe Daddy won't take Cassie to Momma's grave today. Maybe he'll forget.

I met Spike at the Country Club where I use to work part time for Accounts Receivable, four years ago. I liked that job. Little air-conditioned office with my desk by the window where I'd watch the golfers. Not like now, at the steel place, with no windows. At least it's full time.

Spike came in one afternoon with a fuss about his paycheck.

"Belinda does payroll. She's gone for the day," I told him.

"Well, maybe I'd rather talk to you anyhow," he said, sitting on my desk. His curly hair was caught up in a hairnet like all the kitchen help.

"What's your name?" he asked me.

"Ronnie."

"That's a boy's name. But you sure don't look like no boy to me."

"Bet you say that to all the girls working here."

"What're you doing after work?"

"Nothin'."

"Meet me at The Brewery. Six o'clock." He got up and stopped in the doorway. "Name's Spike."

I told Momma I had a date. Not to wait up. She'd looked up from her cutting board, her arthritic hands fumbling with the carrot and knife. I stopped and tried to take the knife from her.

"Momma, let me do that! Why don't you make Daddy help you?"

She'd smiled at me. "Honey, just go on. Have some fun, for a change."

In my mind she's still a saint. I know she wasn't a saint, I know it. Nobody's a saint. Lately, Daddy acts like she was one. Like it's gonna do any good now.

How long is this guy gonna stand here? I hear the bee buzzing again. A wild crazy whine. Like it's injured. It's whizzing around the inside of the car. Maybe it smells my Coke. I pour a little drop on the open window slot. C'mon bee. Here's the way out.

I push off the car and start walking. There's a loud insect racket in my head, and I look back to see if the bee's come out, following my Coke. The guy's still there, but he's looking in the window. I left my keys in the seat where Spike threw them. Maybe I should go back, take the keys so the guy won't take the car. But I don't think he will, and I don't want to go back.

The whirring in my head is making it so I can't think straight. I keep walking, through the entry gate, past the portable toilets. Straight for the Tavern tent. I hear Spike's laugh before I see him. I'd recognize that laugh anywhere, even through the buzzing in my brain.

"Misty," I say. She whips her head around and does a little jump from Spike's lap, but then slowly sits back down, perches herself between his legs. Spike stops laughing. There's a group of them at the table, their faces red and shiny, eyes glassy. They're all quiet, looking at me.

"Let's go," I say to Spike, but I don't touch him or move any closer.

Spike picks up his beer, takes a sip, wipes his mouth with the back of his hand. Misty settles into Spike's lap like she's gonna grow roots there. So, at least I'm not crazy, not sad just because it's the end of the month.

Misty pushes her ice cream scoop breasts at me. "You just go on."

I stare at the blue velvet ribbon around her neck. It's sweat-stained nearly black over her throat at the pulse point.

"You've got responsibilities, Spike." I look up from Misty's throat into her bloodshot eyes. "We've got a daughter."

"So you say," Misty fires and sends more roots down into Spike. Someone behind her snickers.

My legs feel weak. He's trottin' it out again, his dog and pony show about Cassie not being his. There's an insect storm in my head, so powerful I think my head might pop off and fly away.

"Don't start," I hear myself say over the din.

Spike puts his arm around Misty's waist.

"Do the math," he says. Misty smiles.

I can see in their faces they've all been doing Spike's math. The drunken figures he's been formulating more and more often, I'm realizing. Like he's starting to believe it, as if the repetition of the equation somehow gives it a truthful shape.

"Ha. Ha," I'd said, the first time he'd thrust it at me.

"Do the math," he'd insisted. "I mean I'm good and all, but getting you pregnant the first poke? The very first poke?"

"Not funny Spike," I'd said, my fingers going numb where they rested on my stomach.

And then, after Cassie was born, he'd snuck it out again, like a fist he'd been carrying behind his back. Hit me with it.

"She don't look nothin' like me."

"She's three days old, for God's sake. She don't look like nobody."

"Do the math," he'd said. And handed the baby back to me.

"Spike, it's not funny anymore."

"Not tryin' to be funny."

Momma's dead now, and I can see that he's trying it on for good. Trying it on in public. Looking for likely allies.

"She's your daughter," I say to him at the table filled with his newfound army. One woman at the table won't look at me. Probably sitting there pregnant this very minute, doing her own counting of months. Wondering if her own man's gonna come up with the same first poke equation. But she doesn't speak, and she's my enemy.

Misty's talking again — I see her lips moving through the wing flutter in my face.

"You get on. Got no claim here," she says.

I'll kill her first. And then Spike. No, I'll just wound Spike. 'Cause I need him. 'Cause I can't do it alone. Even if it's just a body with no heart, I need the physical presence to tie me to the earth, to hold me down or I will float away. Need a body to lay its weight over Cassie and me, to assure us that we have substance.

Something cold touches me, and I flinch. It's the guy who brought me a Coke in the parking lot. He's brought me another and tapped the cold bottle on my arm.

"See?" he says and holds out his upturned hat. Inside is a bee. Crawling around on a seam. Quiet and not buzzing. I feel like we're the only three living things in that field. Me, the guy, and the bee.

I take the Coke bottle. Press its cold, slippery surface to my forehead and then the back of my neck.

The guy looks at the bee. "Told you it won't hurt you."

"So, it just flew out."

"But I caught it. Held out my hat and it flew right in."

Spike's released his grip on Misty's waist, is starting to get up. Her hands press his chest, trying to get him to settle.

"Who's your friend?" he says, not fully standing or sitting.

I look at the guy holding the bee in his hat.

"I don't know."

Spike grunts. Lets Misty's hands pull him back down under her.

"Name's John," the guy says. I'm not sure who he's telling this to, but the weight of the sound in the air is a solid thing it seems, and I steady myself with it. Know it might be the only clear memory I take from this place.

Looking at Spike, I can't recognize his face anymore because I'm playing a movie in my mind. Where I'm piling all his clothes and things in a heap at the end of the driveway. Leaving a note on them. *Do the Math*. Then I'm taking Cassie by the hand and belting her in the car and driving away, down past the cemetery and far into the country to a new, little yellow house with shutters where I pull in the driveway and tell Cassie "go on and play while I fix dinner."

I'm standing back at the car outside the Faire fence and can't remember even walking here. The keys are still in the front seat.

"How long will it take?" It's John. He's followed me. Maybe he's asking me about the drive to Texarkana. Or when the bee will decide to fly out of his hat, which he still holds in front of him. Or maybe something else.

"Don't know," I say.

He looks at me. Shakes his hat. The bee zips out, with no interest anymore in my car or the field with clover or even its cousins in the trees. Just flies straight off, fast and silent. Disappears. I can't tell where it's gone.

"Well," I say.

"Flew off. Just like that," John says.

I get in my car and start it. Turn the air conditioner on full blast but leave the windows down. John steps away from the car, and I can see him fully and the long shadow he casts behind him. He lights up a cigarette.

"I never forget a face." He says this loudly, and I can hear it over the air conditioner. The hat's back on his head.

"Don't forget mine," I call. He nods. And I know he won't. No matter how old I get, no matter what happens to me, I know this man won't forget my face. It is enough to get me back on the road.

MIDSUMMER
John Knoepfle

the year creaking on its axle
bonfires for lovers and those
afraid of the dark
the year already halfway
my eighty-sixth beyond belief

all you elves and spirits
my life so long unwinding
you opened my mother's eyes
and once I saw them closing
saints and angels wrap her in starlight
and lead her home

all friends all cousins all uncles
all perky aunts and grandparents
walk with us this solstice
when the sun hesitates
then takes its downward course

I have seen on this night
a festival of fireflies
my friend from Iran
had no name for them
called them butterflies with lights

now I want to make an ending
how to do this let the mind
come to some still place
beyond its fret and posturing
where there is no sound

find in the silence after midnight
a sanctuary of light

UNWINTERING
Lauren Schmidt

On the last day of winter I watched a frog
unlock its death in a bed of once-red leaves
flecked with mud and amber shards of light.

It thawed out in one even note
drummed from its pitch fork the way they do
when they come back in spring: spongy,

soft with life, croaking their songs
which sound almost beautiful.

I thought of you as a child in that house
where you learned to freeze against yourself

so he, your winterer, would leave your quilted leaves
unturned long enough until spring, so maybe
you could come back again. But there are those cracks,

as in ice — sprawled out like fingers on your skin — scars
you opened all over yourself to release your body's heat.

I thought of you as a child in that bed of tears
and blood divided from your skin, where soon,

a child will divide from you.

You are frozen on the outside, still,
but your cell, your womb, still warm, and waiting.
You will come back to life when you deliver it,
when she is pulled from the bed of your blood-flesh,

spongy, soft with life, croaking her song:
her reminder of your return.

THE VOODOO DOLL PARADE
Lauren Schmidt

The day just escapes its yellow when we voodoo dolls assemble.

No papier-mâché monsters-on-wheels, no barbershop quartets,
no marching bands, banners, no beauty queens in sashes

cup hand waving from the shoulders of Chevys. Just us,
jumbled together, forming lines to the sound of guffaws.

We're ready-made relics crafted for ritual: our canvas skin
cinched around the cross of two sticks, cherry ice pop crucifix;

Spanish moss muscles our stuffing. They sewed X's for eyes,
Frankensteined our smiles, sutured our mouths to scars that can't deny.

When the marching begins, we sprout their pins like sea urchins.

We're barbed St. Sebastians, or Christmas-bulbed trees.
We're grandmother's coatbreast snaggled with broaches.

We're maps of waged war, or holiday destinations.
We're bull's-eyes in dive bars staggered with hits.

We're punctured to tables when cholera's set in.
We're beds of squashed poppies where the heart pretends to be.

There will be purpling at the injection sites: we all wince in the ills
others wish for us and no one's disinvited, unasked for, allowed to leave.

Such permissive skin: wisps of silver spring from our hearts, our spines,
our X's-for-eyes. And inside, our human stitch unravels.

LARKIN DYING
Stephen Berg

It's quite possible I said to myself
that Larkin died alone except for nurses;
a few friends must have dropped in though to chat,
brought flowers, candy, gossiped, then "My God
it's almost 5 ..." and he in his clean bed
tilted up near the middle and one wide
window that doesn't open: through its glass
hospital buildings, a church tower, treetops,
the insidious scrim of twilight suddenly there
making the white steeple dim, the trees
hardly visible dark green; he hears *Stat*,
chatter, rushing wheels, as someone flat-lined
with paddles is shocked back into existence
Larkin listening, the picture window black.

A STROLL
Stephen Berg

Back lawn a shed a clothesline disappears
into a copse of immense blackish trees —
near-instantly I'll never be seen again
eat dinner with my girls or son-in-laws or friends
stretch out in a beach chair by the eerie
half-excavated pool
square miniature yellow flags on sticks outlining it
to warn someone — do I belong anywhere?
the sky is pierced by an assassin's needle
right through the humdrum fact of nothingness
and rock and soil and dense manicured bushes —
I reach out to one to be sure where
I am and grab some of its leaves
the backhoe's dim huge scoop folded under

THE BABY JARS, MUSEUM OF SCIENCE AND INDUSTRY, 1980
Robin Silbergleid

This summer of roller coasters and Renaissance fairs,
her mother is pregnant
with a baby brother no bigger
than a few grains of rice, a piece of macaroni.
She's the big girl, the big sister,
holding her daddy's hand
as they walk through the submarine
pressed against so many bodies
she can't breathe. She's never been so afraid
in seven years, lured down a coal mine
by the fuzzy chicks incubating in the foyer.
All the kids crowd around, watching them
peck through their shells, emerging
wet and matted, their eyes droopy,
uncertain. A few hours under lamp light
they start to fluff up, and she wonders
how long it took her to look normal —
a preemie in an Isolette, parents
peering at her like a science experiment
though tinted glass. Upstairs,
daddy lifts her up so she can see
the jar babies, their pickled and waxy skin
like the skin on her dolls, with pinpricks
where she tried to pierce their ears.
The two-month embryo is hardly bigger
than her pinky finger, the five-month fetus
as long as her face. And at the end,
in the second-to-the-last case, there's one
at thirty-four weeks, the size she was
when yellow topaz became her birthstone
instead of her mother's garnet. Its eyelids
are fused golden-gray, its mouth pursed.
And she wonders if it wants to be held
the way her mother held her,
as if she were molded of porcelain not bone,
a hand-painted miniature ready to crack.

RUNNING INTO NARCISSUS IN DOWNTOWN CHICAGO

Chris Hayes

He was mirror shopping
in a gold-lit boutique

off Michigan Avenue.
Through the store window,
I recognized the delicate

petal of a face I knew
years ago in college.

When he walked outside
with a gilded, hand mirror
held to his slender chin,

I whispered *Narcissus*
just loud enough

to draw his attention.
We had a drink or two.
I've changed, he said.

That lie dripped down
his tongue like molasses.

Here he was, dressed
in a tailored cashmere
overcoat, his fluid name

stitched in gold script
above the inside pocket.

*You can have anything
customized in Korea.
Look at this lettering!*

As we left the bar,
his tall body bowed

like a stalk of hemlock.
I spoke, and he drifted,
fixing those blue eyes

on a nearby reflection of
the flesh that cursed him.

Even if the image was
curved or distorted,
he kept staring. He kept

sizing himself up
for the next new vase.

— *with gratitude to O. Hopkins*

THE POINT AT WHICH CROOKED LINES CROSS *Fiction*
A. N. Teibe

Nicola hadn't recognized him at first. The beard and shaggy hair threw her. "Hey — Nicola!" he'd said as they approached each other on the trail. She'd been running along the river every day since she got into town, filling up on the experience before heading back to Cincinnati, where she had everything ready for the move. She'd endured the rises and falls, the detours, but she was headed to the East Coast — to New York — for good. The river trail and surrounding mountains were something she'd miss about Granton, Idaho, but they wouldn't be enough to lure her back.

And he had frightened her with a smile she thought was meant to disarm, so she'd hesitate, not follow the instincts of self-protection: scream, sprint away, jab fingernails in his eyes, or shove a knee to his crotch. The years living away had overcome her childhood training to be polite. She didn't share the locals' sense of security anymore — their idea of being sheltered in this Rocky Mountain town.

And good thing, she thought, relieved, that he had seen the unchecked second of fear on her face as he'd stepped in front of her and put his hands on her shoulders so she'd stop. Good thing, because otherwise he'd have seen another reaction, involuntary and impulsive, cross her face: one of delight and desire, obscured quickly by the mask of forced composure, but belied by a subsequent spell of nervous chatter. *Oh, hi. How long has it been? You're looking good. Imagine running into you here. Did I say running? Ha! That's funny.* Nicola was also glad she'd been running the trail hard; the effects of adrenaline shearing through her — her voice catching when she spoke, her pounding heart — might be mistaken by him as the result of intense exercise.

"Nicola Sampson. I'm sorry. I scared you," he said.

"It's the beard; I didn't recognize you." She was staring, taking him in. Simultaneously searching for and finding the victorious smile and face of the high school quarterback he'd been.

"You must be in town for the reunion. Where is it you live now? St. Louis?" He made no move to continue up the trail, but had set his legs wide and folded his arms across his chest. Settling in for a conversation.

"Close, Cincinnati." Nicola felt out of body and was surprised to realize the sensation hadn't happened because she was talking to Joel Beck, but because having this conversation was so real and natural — different than the way she'd felt in high school. The woman she'd become was speaking with him and felt in easy control. And then she said, "What reunion?"

Nicola had sat on the dry fountain's tiled ledge and wondered how she'd gotten herself into this. She had no idea when the bus she wanted was coming and hadn't seen another female in the twenty minutes that she'd been in this Mexican, dirt-paved village. She felt the men watching her, wondering what the gringa was doing there. They sat at open-air restaurant tables drinking beer and scooping up chile with tortillas. Leaned against walls, day's work done, hats tipped down against the afternoon sun. Moved slowly, arcing their path of travel around her just enough as they passed, their "ch-ch-ch-ch-ch" low. Subdued. Not like the loud, but harmless calls that she routinely met leaving the metro station on her way to the language institute. She smiled to herself, remembering her early days in the country. How those cat calls had made her feel noticed, singled out amid the hugeness of Mexico City — until she'd observed the way they were distributed without discretion to every passing woman. That had felt the same, somehow, as never being noticed in Granton.

Bluffing confidence, Nicola sat tall and pretended to read her travel guide. A casual glance down, and she saw dust from the road clinging to her shiny black loafers. It reminded her of Simon and renewed her feelings of insignificance. She hated the weight of the irony, reliving that shame here, in this no-name village not even mentioned in the travel guide. But the bus driver had been adamant. *Here*, he'd said as he let her off. *Wait here. You can get a bus to el D.F. here.*

In an hour it would start to get dark. Nicola hummed the tune and thought the words. *Bring me out of my distress ... keep my soul and deliver me.* It had become a habit after so many years of use, an automatic response.

She had not come to town for the reunion, but to sell her parents' house. Renting it out from Cincinnati had been enough of a pain. From New York it would be worse. She had no reason to keep the house, anyway. She'd never live in Granton again, and the sale would make a down payment possible in the city. But she had known her high school reunion would fall in the three weeks she'd scheduled to be in town. The invitation had born Granton's predictably innocent excitement: *It's been twenty years! Isn't it time?* The peppy energy and optimism seemed like one of the cheers led all those years ago by the high school spirit squad.

Nicola had been counting on an old friend to be her date for the reunion: Perry Schwab, known during high school as "the gay boy from Granton." But he had taken off to Puerto Rico to teach yoga at a resort. *Permanently*, his mother had told Nicola over the phone. *Do you want his address?*

Perry had been there for Nicola at the senior prom. It had been Perry's idea, but Nicola went along gladly, the joke covering her needy desire to attend and be seen at the dance. She'd worn a tux and a mascara mustache, he a floofy gown and tiara — both of them emboldened by having each other as a date and their need to make a larger statement, *I'm just an interloper here.*

After the news of Perry's move, Nicola toyed with the idea of calling one of the girls she'd been friends with growing up, but though a girls' night out might work in a city, all her Granton friends had married years ago and become mothers of the first-rate, small-town kind. She admired their family-life success, but hadn't kept in touch with any of them since her parents had both died, leaving the house as her only tie to Granton, as the only reason to visit. Going with a no-risk date to the senior prom wasn't the same as attaching herself at an awkward angle to a married couple she hardly knew anymore.

New Year's Eve, 1981. Nicola had forgotten whose dimly lit basement it had taken place in — the first boy-girl party of eighth grade. Some boys had brought peach schnapps and already had a buzz. A series of 45's played on a stereo. Circles of girls huddled together, alternately looking over their shoulders and turning back to whisper. Couples bear-hugged on the dance floor to the slow songs, and talk was spreading that a few of them had left the main room altogether to make out, staking private claim to the home's downstairs bedrooms. But most of the kids hung around the big open room, eating chips and talking, teasing each other, daring their friends to ask someone to dance. He had pulled Nicola away from the group.

"Where are we going?" she said as he led her to a dark hallway between the bedrooms.

"Hey, it's New Year's Eve, Nicola. You can't ring it in without a kiss."

Yvonne had been Nicola's favorite Sunday school teacher. When she and her ten-year-old son had moved into town it was big news. Divorced. That was one thing, but Yvonne's looks got Nicola the most. Her big hoop earrings that belonged on a hooker according to the other women in town. Her long, curly permed hair, gold and silver with highlights. Her name, Yvonne. Sophisticated and glamorous. Not a Granton name at all. Not Shirley or Susan. Not Barbara. Not Mrs. anything, even to the kids in her class at church.

About a year after moving in, she had taught the children a song she composed, based on the 25th Psalm. Nicola remembered standing with the rest of her Sunday school class on the sanctuary's elevated podium, singing Yvonne's arrangement for the whole congregation during an Easter Sunday worship service.

The troubles of my heart are enlarged.
Turn thee unto me and have mercy upon me.
Show me thy ways, for I am desolate and afflicted.
Look upon mine affliction and my pain.
Bring me out of my distress and deliver me,
For I wait on thee.

Yvonne accompanied them on the guitar. That had never been done before. Their church used an organ only — that was it — but Yvonne had convinced the pastor somehow, and there she was, unafraid of the talk that would follow, her hoop earrings swaying as she tossed her head of hair around, strumming along with the children's voices. How serious and lonely Nicola thought the song was. According to the printed program, the song was supposed to be heard as a reflection on Christ's followers after his death before the glorious resurrection. But Nicola thought it meant more. That it was about how living in Granton must be for Yvonne. Nicola asked if she would teach her how to play the accompaniment. *I feel just like you*, Nicola wanted to say. *I can tell from the song.*

Throughout the lessons at Yvonne's house, Nicola watched and tried to match Yvonne's nimble working of the strings and frets along the guitar's neck. As they practiced playing the song, Yvonne would talk to Nicola about the places she'd lived and people she'd known. Whether the memories were good or bad, Yvonne found a way to relate them to her idea of faith. "God's word can be interpreted in many ways. It's big enough to fit every need." Being with Yvonne, Nicola felt a lightness of relief. Messages that once had alienated her became free of condemnation and full of comfort.

"Hey listen," Joel said to Nicola as they ran down the trail together. He'd decided to join her for the rest of her run. "How about we grab lunch. Can you drive? My truck's getting lubed." He said it so naturally. As if it were nothing. *Joel Beck asking her on a date.*

"I don't have my car either, Joel. I jogged from my parents' place."

She'd trained for and regularly run half-marathons the last eight years and couldn't resist the impulse to kick into a quicker pace, confident that she could wind Joel. It would be fun to show up the superstar. The river embankment was steep from seasons of high water erosion, and the trail narrowed, forcing them close together.

"No problem." Joel smiled, breathing hard. "I've got my mountain bike chained at the trailhead. I can get us there." He nudged her shoulder with his and winked. "It'll be like a date."

Trusting three years of high school Spanish, Nicola left for Mexico City the summer after graduation. Living there would be cheap, and the few thousand bucks she'd saved from working weekends at the movie theater would go a lot further than at some out-of-town university. She would study at a language institute, rent a room, and travel. Granton Technical College hadn't been an option at all. Nicola would not go to GTC to learn phlebotomy, nurse assisting, bookkeeping, or any of the other non-professions offered there. They all led to one thing: staying in Granton forever as an underpaid nothing.

Some kids headed to find work in one of the west's upstart cities: Seattle, Denver, Salt Lake City — even Las Vegas — as though that were as far as their imaginations could take them. No one even mentioned Los Angeles. Nicola knew better. She'd spent the last five years growing in quiet rebellion against small-town limitations and the West's lack of experience with the cosmopolitan ideals she read about in magazines and books and which she'd seen in movies at the theater. The only city that counted was New York.

In the beginning, the attention Nicola got in Mexico City had made her feel important. The family she stayed with had taken her to a neighborhood street festival the week she moved in, and she'd been flattered by the stream of dance partners — little boys to married men — who took turns leading her to the mariachi music played by a band of musicians.

She hadn't foreseen but came to appreciate the influx of attention she got for being a foreigner. The language institute's evening conversation classes gave her access to a circle of acquaintances eager to act as guides, familiarizing Nicola with the city and inviting her to parties and discotheques.

He had eased her against the hallway wall, then smiled and said, "Happy New Year, Nicola." The music and conversation seemed far away as he leaned close, supported by one arm placed just above her left ear. The hair on her neck prickled warm, and then his mouth was on hers, soft and open. It seemed like a second, and it seemed like forever. Nicola's mind tried to keep up — *What should I do? What should I do?* — but she kissed him back, met his tongue without effort, with pleasure. When he pulled away, Nicola was breathless. Her first kiss. Joel Beck! She couldn't get a word out of her mouth.

When school resumed, the hallways buzzed with stories of the party. A friend told Nicola about the contest, how it had been the result of a Truth or Dare game at the party.

"A bunch of guys were competing to see who could kiss the most girls." Joel Beck had won. By midnight, he'd kissed twelve. "And he saved Tiffany Watson for last. She's the lucky dog who got the real kiss at midnight."

He'd kissed Nicola at ten-thirty.

It was during one of Nicola's guitar lessons that she noticed Yvonne's eyes. "Yvonne," she said, "your eyes look yellow." Yvonne's eyes brimmed. It seemed as though she wanted to say something, but Nicola guessed that her words had gotten caught in the thick dryness that comes from trying to hold back tears.

"What's wrong?" Nicola felt inadequate. What she had said made Yvonne cry. How was she supposed to cover this mistake? "Don't worry. You look okay. You're always pretty."

"Oh, Nicola," Yvonne said. "That's not it. I know they look yellow." She paused. "Can I tell you why?" That Nicola wasn't to tell anyone else seemed implicit.

"What are you doing, woman!" Joel said, rubbing the skin of his knee that had gotten chaffed in the fall.

They'd made it to the house Nicola grew up in. Balancing on someone's bicycle handlebars was harder on the rear than Nicola remembered. She'd struggled not to throw off Joel's balance, and the two of them had laughed their guts out as he pedaled them unsteadily along, trusting Nicola's directions as she navigated the turns and gutter bumps for him. They'd crashed on the sidewalk just outside the house because Nicola had reached out to grab a cluster of orange berries from the mountain ash growing in the strip of lawn between the sidewalk and gutter.

"Just getting you back," Nicola said, throwing the berries one by one at his head. She'd jumped from the handlebars just in time, "for all the berries you chucked at me when I used to walk past your house on my way home from school." She had always dreaded and cherished the frequent assaults. She'd felt singled out, chosen. "Remember, you and your mom had this same kind of tree."

"When was that, fifth grade? Man, those babies could fly." He tossed a berry up and swat-batted it into the street.

"Fourth, fifth, sixth. You pretty much tormented me from the time you moved in until junior high."

She saw now. *He'd just been a little boy, living in the thrill of making a girl get mad and watching her cry.*

Joel lay back on the lawn, propped himself up with an elbow, and started to pick the scattered berries off the grass, lobbing them back at Nicola. "Do you remember," he asked her, grinning, "what happened at senior prom?"

"How could I forget? I almost didn't get to walk at graduation because of it."

She met them on the bus from Oaxaca to the state of Chiapas, where she was planning to visit the jungle ruins of Palenque. Kevin asked if he could sit by her. "You're British," Nicola said as she moved her bag off the seat. His friend passed the two of them and took a seat behind in the next row. Nicola could tell this Kevin guy was going to come on strong, but that was okay; she was bored and happy to talk with somebody in English. But his friend was the one with the looks. Sun-streaked, disheveled light brown hair. A warm tan. One slightly crooked tooth that made him real.

Kevin started in just as she'd predicted, talking nonstop, touching her arm to emphasize points, openly tracing his gaze along her torso as they talked. On the bus and in the towns between Mexico City and Oaxaca, Nicola had seen the way wandering foreign travelers allied themselves with partners quickly and a come-and-go attitude. The ride was going to be long to Chiapas where she'd change buses for Palenque, and she didn't have it in her to be rude, so she went along and acted interested.

"What are you reading?" she said, gesturing to the book that had been sitting in Kevin's lap.

"Garcia Marquez."

"I haven't heard of it. Is it good?"

"That's the author." Kevin's pause of disbelief wasn't lost on her. "Gabriel Garcia Marquez. *One Hundred Years of Solitude.*" Another pause. "He won the Nobel Prize in literature."

She felt Granton cling to her like an ugly, unwanted friend, conspicuous and degrading. Hard to be shed of, like husky hair on a black sweater. Nicola didn't say that she hadn't heard of Garcia Marquez, but determined to buy a copy of the book and decided right then that Kevin was never going to touch her.

After the bus's twenty-minute beer and bathroom break in a small town, Nicola re-boarded after the two guys and sat next to Kevin's friend, Simon.

"Are you going to San Cristóbal with us?" he said in a German accent, an easy grin on his face.

"Is that where you guys are headed?" *San Cristóbal de las Casas.* Nicola had already rejected the idea of heading to the highland town and surrounding Mayan villages. More than one travel book had issued the warning for visitors to the area: *Women should dress modestly and are expected to cover shoulders, arms, and legs.* Nicola hadn't come to Mexico to deal with that kind of stuff. Unbelievably, Simon chose to change buses at the next junction and head to Palenque with her, rather than continue on to San Cristobal with Kevin. As they walked down the bus aisle to get off, Nicola looked back and saw Kevin looking wounded and betrayed.

Spotlights rested on the Olympics-style award podiums at the front of the ballroom. The prom royalty runners-up had taken their places and received flowers and crowns.

"And now," the school principal announced into the microphone, "the class of 1985's senior prom queen ..."

Perry rushed up in his dress and tilting tiara, hands pressed to his cheeks, his shrieks of joy overshadowing the winner's name. "I won! I won! I knew I would. Let me die and go to heaven now!"

Nicola watched as the real prom queen's face fell to shock and changed to anger. She ran to the principal, screaming. "Get that fag off my throne. I earned this moment. He's ruining the most important event of my life!"

Nicola and Perry got kicked out of the dance and suspended from school. On Monday, talk flew through the high school halls that the prom queen's mother was going to sue.

Joel's kiss had kept Nicola going through her largely un-kissed high school years. She hadn't told anyone about that New Year's Eve, but hung on to it, embarrassed and possessive at the same time, forcing herself to feign disinterest as Joel's athletic talent thrust him to the forefront of both the school's and the community's attention.

As a sophomore he started as quarterback for the varsity football team. One game had been enough for Nicola. Sitting on the bleachers, she watched with anticipation as the team ran to the field from the locker room at the start of the game. Number twelve. There he was, and then behind her, a girl's voice, "Oooh, look at how hot Joel Beck looks in those tight pants." A wave of agreeing sentiment swept through the surrounding female spectators. Nicola felt excited and proud. Joel had talked to her that afternoon at his mom's house. She and Yvonne had been in the kitchen, decorating cupcakes they'd made for the booster club to sell at the game.

"Nice work, ladies," he said, stepping between them and wrapping his arms around their shoulders. "Did you make these just for me?"

Every one of them.

And then he'd turned to Nicola and looked at her. A dance was scheduled after every home game. *She could find him there, and they could talk.* As he headed out the door he said, "Cheer loud for me tonight, Nicola."

On the bleachers behind her, a girl whispered to a friend, "I heard he made it with Tiffany Watson after last week's victory dance. If we win, you know who's going to be busy tonight."

Nicola got up and left, joining the crowd that hung around the periphery of the games but didn't actually watch them.

Unable to sleep, she'd whisper parts of the psalm in bed at night as she thought about Joel — imagining him lying there by her, as the one she talked to, the one whose touch would bless her with relief from dry desolation. *Show me thy ways.* The kiss had started an aching agitation in her body. *Turn thee unto me.* Nicola yearned for it run its course, up the willing incline. *Bring me out of my distress and deliver me.* To the peak of the precipice.

They decided to stay at the house and ordered pizza. Joel's idea. Nicola got a blanket, and they sat on the lawn, waiting for it to arrive. Joel picked at the grass.

"Thanks for what you did for my mom. I was so full of myself back then I didn't even notice everything that was happening to her." He'd been looking at the ground, but lifted his head toward Nicola and reached out to tap her hand. "I know she liked having you come around."

Joel still had it. The smile, the effortless flirting manner. *He could still have his pick.* Age had started to etch a subtle sunburst of lines from the outside corners of his eyes. When he squinted against the sun his skin puckered there. It made him look like a river rafting guide.

Hepatitis C had made Yvonne's eyes yellow. For a while the disease's slow progression hadn't revealed the other symptoms and complications that would follow — GI bleeding, coughing up blood. That had started around the time Nicola left for Mexico. The bouts of ascites came a few years after that when Nicola was in college at Hall Field in Cincinnati. Yvonne's belly would fill with fluid, expanding her abdomen like a pregnancy, stretching the skin uncomfortably tight.

On a visit to Granton during a semester recess, Nicola had gone with her to get it drained. In the car Yvonne joked. "Just what a forty-three-year-old, divorced woman needs, to look pregnant in this town. And it comes back every six months. People must think I'm keeping pretty busy."

But everyone knew by then about the hepatitis, and plenty of time had been spent wondering how Yvonne had contracted it.

Most of the other foreign students from the language institute had chosen Acapulco for their three-week vacation. Beaches, nightlife, the party. Nicola wanted to visit ruins and see real Mexican life. She'd originally allotted only a few days for the Caribbean Sea, and rather than deal with the commotion of Cancun, Nicola planned to stay on small, underdeveloped Isla Mujeres. But she and Simon were having a lot of fun together, so she wanted to get to its white beaches sooner — to lie by him in the powder-soft sand and eat sweetened, cinnamon-spiced arroz con leche in the mornings.

After Palenque, they'd stopped at the waterfalls of Agua Azul and decided to spend the afternoon swimming in the pools of some of the gentler falls before heading north to the colonial city Merida. Nicola was surprised how easily the connection with Simon had come. They'd horsed around in the water, splashing each other and joining an impromptu chicken fight tournament with other tourists. When Nicola got knocked off his shoulders, Simon led her to a shallow area shaded by an overhang of rocks. He put his palms at her hips and leaned in to kiss her. His fingers drummed the skin of her back. Nicola shivered as they necked in the warm water. Later, on the bus to Merida, they took turns telling stories about their past and singing country music songs because Simon had a fascination with them. When Simon took a nap, Nicola watched him, sleeping slumped against the bus window. She touched one of his eyebrows and traced its shape with her finger. If things went right, maybe he'd come to Mexico City with her, and she could introduce him to everyone.

"Why are you telling me this?" Nicola wanted to say to her mother during one of her weekly phone calls to Mexico from the States. But Nicola had asked.

"Well, Yvonne was down getting her hair done, and the hairdresser had to stop right in the middle of touching up her roots and take her to the hospital. She'd stopped drinking that medicine that was supposed to take the ammonia out of her blood because it was making her have diarrhea all the time. She didn't want to be like that for the wedding."

"What wedding? What happened to Yvonne, Mom?"

"Joel's. I've never seen anybody acting so wacko. She was sitting in the stylist's chair talking to people that weren't there. They had to postpone the wedding, but what difference does a week make when a little one's already on the way?"

"Joel? He's getting married?" Nicola assumed he'd be marrying Tiffany Watson.

But, her mother told her, Tiffany had dumped Joel after falling for a basketball recruit from the technical college. "Pretty soon he was dating Nancy Lewis, and not long after, that young lady got pregnant."

Nancy Lewis. She was two years younger than Joel and Nicola. She was still in high school. Nicola immediately wished she'd given in to Simon back in Isla Mujeres.

Joel brought it up again. "So, the reunion. Are you going?"

"I don't know." *I wanted to, because after I sell my parent's house I'm never coming back.* She'd planned on the reunion being the back cover to a book she'd been forced to read. "What about you?"

"Same thing. I thought about it but ..." Joel looked over his shoulder as though someone were there.

"What?"

He turned back to Nicola. "When I moved to Jackson, I finally felt like I was my own man. Making things work on my terms. I feel like going to the reunion might somehow mess that up."

"You live in Jackson Hole now? You didn't say that."

"Yeah, about nine years now. After Nancy and I got divorced. That whole thing was a mess from the get-go. When you have a kid, though, it's hard to break away."

"I always saw you living in Granton forever. You know, Joel Beck, everybody's favorite guy."

"Yeah. Where did that get me?"

"So what are you doing now?" Nicola asked.

"I have this cabin I built outside Jackson." Nicola could see the happiness in his eyes. He looked like a kid daydreaming. "I build for other people, mostly vacation homes, and fish the rest of the time." He locked on Nicola's eyes and didn't glance away. "You should come visit. You'd love it."

She admired Joel's arms. The sleeves of his T-shirt fit tightly around his biceps. Senior year, his 265-pound, six-rep bench press record had been tacked to the P.E. bulletin board along with other players' personal bests. How many times Nicola had lingered outside the weight room to read it, hoping to run into Joel. Wanting him to look at her again.

"Maybe I will."

They were eating dinner at an open-air café facing Merida's main plaza when Simon recognized a small group of Swiss tourists he'd crossed paths with before. They had the earthy look of well-traveled backpackers. The women were tan, makeup-free, and wore their hair short or in ponytails. The colors of their clothes were subdued. Baggy, khaki shorts and pants. Their silk-screened T-shirts gray or washed-out reds and blues. A few of them joined Simon and Nicola at the table. She didn't care that they spoke German to one another, knowing how egocentric it would be to expect them to talk in English.

He was still talking with two of the Swiss women when Nicola decided to head back to the hostel where she and Simon were staying. The mosquitoes were biting, and Nicola was bored, but Simon and the others were laughing and drinking their coffee. She wanted to get to bed anyway, because the bus for Isla Mujeres was going to leave early the next morning. As Nicola stood to go, she saw one of the women look her up and down and say something to Simon.

"She thinks you dress like a little girl," Simon said. Nicola looked down at herself, then over at the smiling woman. It wasn't a friendly smile. "It's true," Simon said. "Look at your shoes. And your little skirt. You're dressed like a schoolgirl."

Nicola didn't look at her own shoes, but at the woman's: suede, cork-soled shoes with a thick strap at the heel. Well-worn. Back at the hostel, Nicola felt spiteful. Her shiny, pointy-toed black loafers and pink miniskirt had done fine every weekend in the strobes and pulsing crowds of the clubs off Avenida Insurgentes in Mexico City. *Where it counts,* Nicola wanted to say, although she wasn't sure she really believed it.

They got to Isla Mujeres early enough to eat and take a scooter ride around the island's perimeter at dusk. Simon took the curves fast and was starting to scare Nicola. "You're going to kill us!" she yelled, but the air rushed down her throat and muffled the words. That morning she hadn't been sure Simon was going to get up and go with her. Before the thing with the Swiss tourist, Nicola had imagined Simon asking if he could stay on with her when she headed back to Mexico City.

The next day they hung out at the beach and played pickup volleyball with whoever was willing. After ceviche for lunch, they lounged in the water, sitting along the sea floor's gradual slope, submerged to their hips in the quiet surf. Simon traced a finger along Nicola's belly, following the line of her bikini top across her body, down the side of her torso, turning across again at her waistband. His finger lingered there, slowly moving back and forth. Nicola's heart hammered, and it was hard to breathe. Her awareness focused on Simon's touch and the heat that she felt growing. He moved his finger to the other side of her waist and continued drawing smaller and smaller squares toward the center of her abdomen. At her bellybutton he paused, then pressed it and whispered, "Pow."

It should have been just another one of the every-six-months pericentesis to drain Yvonne's belly. But a small, accidental nick to her bowel did a lot of damage, releasing infection in the belly. Nicola listened over the phone from her office at Hall Field while her mother told the sequence of events as she'd heard them from a neighbor who worked as a nurse at the hospital. A few days after getting drained, Yvonne had gotten a fever, and she had belly pain even though the fluid was gone. "She went into shock. They put tubes down her throat for a breathing machine. She never woke up. Her heart just stopped."

Nicola cried and said it for them both. *The troubles of my heart are enlarged.* Yvonne had taught her that those words fit any situation.

Bring me out of my distress. That they could bring relief, rather than distance and damnation. *Look upon mine affliction and my pain.* Nicola had made it so far out of Granton and was doing fine where she was. Yvonne's pain had ended. Why didn't Nicola feel as if the prayer had been answered? *I wait on thee.* Her faith felt withered.

Simon had stood and headed up the beach. "Come on, Nicola."
"Where are we going?"
"You'll see."
He rented a thatched cabana with privacy panels at the top of the beach. Inside, they lay kissing, the warm, fine-grained sand along Nicola's back. Simon's hands worked up and down her body, then stopped at the hip ties of her bikini. He was teasing, and Nicola playfully brushed his hands away. His fingers became more persistent. "Don't," Nicola said. He had undone one side, and his hand moved down her belly low. She hadn't let her imagination take it this far. Nicola pushed him away. "Stop it Simon." *I don't want to.* She thought he'd get mad, but he lay on his side, smiling, his head propped on his hand.

The next morning, Simon packed his bag and told Nicola he was taking off for Guatemala. She walked with him to the Punta Sam ferry where he exchanged addresses with her in a polite, but dead-end gesture. Nicola took the next ferry three hours later and found herself heading back to Mexico City several days early by way of a bus whose unplanned stop left her sitting on the ledge of a dry fountain in a village whose name she never learned.

"What about you, Nicola?" Joel said, "What've you been up to all these years?"
The line Nicola's life had been since she left Granton hadn't always drawn straight — had even stalled at undesirable junctures — but she had always thought it was going somewhere. And it had. Certain stops stood out. Mexico. Hall Field, the private women's college in Cincinnati that had granted Nicola a language studies scholarship and which had also given her a first taste of professional employment after graduation. After six years, her job recruiting foreign students had led to a fundraising position in the development office. She would never have thought fundraising would take her to the top, but it had. Skill in raising money didn't go unnoticed. And now she'd be in charge. Development chair for a private college in the city. New York City. Over time, Nicola had put less effort put into finding a man and more into work. These days she and her friends lined each other up once in a while, but she'd learned not to expect much.
"Mostly I've been right there in Cincinnati. Eighteen years now."

Nicola laughed. "I guess I've lived there about as long as you've been a dad."

Joel reached out and took hold of Nicola's hands. "That settles it, then. We're going together. The cosmic coincidence of that number is destiny."

His joke made her feel bittersweet. She could see he'd been working up to this — finding a way to get them to the reunion together, once he'd guessed that she, too, didn't have a date. But when she thought about Joel's life, so much of it seemed like a locomotive that plowed ahead at full steam, but hadn't been able to take the curves without jumping the track. There was something he still needed from Granton. Nicola considered letting him follow the path he'd pursued with her throughout the day. Weighed where it would lead them.

But given this chance with him, she had nothing to win. He'd been innocent, unwitting of the years he'd wielded her. She acknowledged the remnant of desire she'd felt in the flutter when he'd stopped her on the trail. His interest in her — finally — was flattering, and Nicola allowed herself a moment of fantasy — transporting this present circumstance to a time when she could have fallen foolishly, greedily to the wash of pleasure that being with Joel would have brought.

HOODLUMS

Fiction

J.R. Angelella

I.

Chucklehead rents an apartment in Brooklyn where Al Capone used to live. He says that Capone's spirit haunts the building.

I say the only spirit that exists is the spirit of Chucklehead's landlord trying to scare up the three months past due rent. I tell him that eviction is a very real thing. That the landlord will not think twice about changing the locks. Put his shit on the street. It's not like he has a car for collateral. Poor bastard.

Chucklehead chews on the end of a stick of pepperoni as he tells me about shit. He tells me that sometimes late at night he can hear Capone whistling in the front hallway near the kitchen. He says he's not sure of the song, but it's in perfect pitch.

I mention to Chucklehead, casually, that Capone didn't die in Brooklyn, but in Florida of syphilis.

He says that when a person dies the spirit doesn't haunt the place where he or she died, but the place where he or she was born.

First, I tell the prick to stop saying *he or she*. Then I double back on our conversation and ask him when he plans on paying his rent again.

Chucklehead tells me that I am arguing semantics.

I ask him where he learned that word.

He tells me to fuggetaboutit.

I ask him if Deirdre has filed the divorce papers yet.

He whistles an unfamiliar ditty, hideously so and out-of-tune.

I tell him that divorce is a means to an end and something he should consider.

He says that Al Capone said the same thing about booze and Prohibition.

II.

His name, in actuality, is Charles, but when we were kids he was given the name Chucklehead. When he'd laugh his whole head would bobble like one of those bobblehead dolls. I would have called him Bobblehead, except that a kid three blocks over already had that name. I have no idea what that kid's real name was or even how he got Bobblehead.

Regardless, an unique identity is important to a child, and to prove all is fair in love and all that bullshit, my nickname came later that year. I drank rotten milk from one of those school issued cartons and threw up all over myself. Chucklehead gave me the name Milk Boy. Chucklehead and Milk Boy, and that was that.

III.

I stand on the bottom step of the stoop to his brownstone building.

Chucklehead locks the front door; turning the knob like a madman, quadruple checking.

"Seriously? It's locked, man."

"It doesn't always."

"You never did answer my question — how are things with Deirdre?"

"You should ask her."

"Where is she staying?"

"Hungry? I'm hungry."

"Did she move out for good? Did she move upstate?"

"I think I want Chinese. I have a hankering for an egg roll."

"Is this, like, a trial thing? What's the word — separation? Or is it dead in the head?"

"Beef with garlic sauce. Won ton soup. And some pork dumplings."

"Deirdre, bro." I clap my hands together. "What is happening with that?"

Chucklehead grabs my shoulder. "Drop it," he says. Then, "Chinese."

IV.

I call Kitty at work to let her know I am eating Chinese with Chucklehead, but her office line is busy. I dial zero for her secretary, the only secretary in the office — Kitty's own business.

"Brooklyn Real Estate Solutions. Good afternoon, this is Jeannine speaking."

Jeannine is a single parent, mother of three, and has been Kitty's secretary for the past three years. I've had more than the casual sexual fantasy about her, so much so, in fact, that I've had to physically stop going in to the office — out of sheer embarrassment that she knows about my fantasy, like she can smell it on me or see it in my face. The fantasies have become annoyingly repetitive, yet somehow not completely predictable. Usually it involves one of those leather sex swings, a leopard print feather duster, and a jar of maraschino cherries with stems. She's not your ideal fantasy bang girl — not terribly tall, not terribly thin, not terribly attractive, stringy hair, and frumpy clothes — but for the past year it's been all about her and uncomfortably often.

"Jeannine. Hello."

Sex swing.

She tells me Kitty's out and won't be back in the office.

Leopard print feather duster.

She tells me Kitty will be calling in for her messages.

Jar of cherries.

She asks if I want to leave a message or try her cell.

With stems.

"Gabe? You there? You want to try her cell?"

"I don't want to bother her. Just tell her that I am thinking about her even on Sundays."

"Even on Sundays?"

"It's a saying. A thing. Something I say," I say. "Just jot it down."

"Will she understand it?"

"She'll expect it."

"When can we expect to see you again? It's been a long time."

Before I have a chance to answer, Chucklehead says, "Nope," and slaps my cell phone out of my hand, the phone bouncing across the sidewalk into the wet gutter.

"If there is an explanation, I'd love to hear it," I say.

"Phone taps."

"Is this that whole Capone thing again?"

"For real." Then, points to the sky. "Satellites."

"Not for real. For fake." I pick up the phone and dry it on my jeans. Jeannine is still talking, but can't figure out what the hell she is going on about, so I say, "Jeannine? Hello? Can you hear me?"

She says, "I can hear you just fine."

Chucklehead reaches for my phone again and, blocking him with a stiff arm, I say, "Jeannine? Hello? Hello? Hello? Why can't she hear me?"

V.

Chucklehead and I work as collections agents for a company in midtown Manhattan — a crumbling four-story building off of Times Square. Our job, as ridiculous as it seems, is to sit in a cubicle and call random people, asking them to pay their hefty debt.

Before lunch, I call a woman who owes eight hundred dollars on her credit card. With lovely diction and a seemingly sweet demeanor, she answers and I ask for a Ms. Templeton. The woman waits a beat before hanging up. I call her back, but the phone goes to voicemail. My message is, resoundingly, three words: Please pay us.

I grab my brown bag lunch — two slices of leftover cheese pizza — and walk to the staff lounge. Chucklehead, who works in the cubicle next to me, follows behind, whistling an unfamiliar tune. He wears a white button-down shirt under a grey pinstriped vest with matching suit pants.

"You look like a New Yorker cartoon?" I say, taking a bite of my slice.

"Look at me when I am talking to you." He towers over me.

"But you didn't say anything."

"What, am I invisible over here? Look at me."

"This is me. Looking at you. And you. Didn't say anything."

Chucklehead laughs, his head bobbling around, his cheeks jiggling like Jell-O. He slaps the pizza from my hand, which hits the table and flips to the carpet, cheese side down. Damn.

Another collections agent and two secretaries look up from their newspapers and magazines. I have never fantasized about either of the secretaries — Carla or Peter. I have tried to fantasize a three-way — Jeannine, Carla and me — but no cigar. Always ends up back on Jeannine — pun intended.

"I said fucking look at my eyes when I talk to you." Chucklehead breathes heavy — garlic and something else. Sardines.

"Like I said, you didn't say anything."

Chucklehead hurdles plastic chairs, like an Olympian, grabs a fistful of my hair and lifts me out of my chair. "I'm going have you and your whole family whacked," he says. "You hear me? WHACKED."

The collections agent drops his sandwich. Peanut butter and jelly. Sad.

The two secretaries freeze and stare.

"This isn't a Scorcese film," I say. "Easy up on the hair, Chucklehead Corleone."

I stomp on his feet until he lets go.

VI.

Peter knocks on the bathroom stall — witness protection — and hands me my slices. Holding both like Lady Justice, I ask him if he knows which one fell on the floor.

"With all due respect," he says. "That's all you want to know?"

VII.

After work, I run into Chucklehead crossing 53rd Street.

"I'll fight back," I say, lifting fists to my face.

"I don't want to fight you."

"I mean it. I'll clock you cold." I shake them.

"Are those your *dukes*?"

"Sledgehammers," I say.

"Look, Milk Boy, I'm sorry. When I woke up this morning, I was Capone," he says, looking around like the FBI was listening. "He must have entered my body while I was asleep."

"If you're Al Capone, you know what that makes me?" I ask. "The ghost of Eliot Ness?"

"Not a joke," he says. "It happened. He entered me."

"Like," I say, making a sexual gesture pumping my hips. "Entered you?"

"Am I a clown? Is this funny?"

"You want my advice? Move to a different apartment," I say. "Maybe one formerly owned by less violent people. Like Martin Luther King or Ghandi. Hell, move in with me and you can become the old man that used to live in my apartment. He owned his own moving company." I lower my sledgehammers. "Don't expect me to start calling you Scarface."

Chucklehead tells me that Capone once killed a man for calling him Scarface.

"Good thing you don't have any scars," I say.

"Let me buy you a coffee," he says. "To make amends."

"Fine," I say. "But no funny business."

In the restaurant, Chucklehead asks for a menu, tapping a finger over the items as he orders. "Eggplant parmesan hero with extra marinara sauce and a side of fried calamari and a quarter-cut of fresh mozzarella." He says *mozzarella*, but sounds like *mootz-a-rell*.

I order an espresso.

"You want the calamari out first or with your hero?" The waitress licks the tip of a pencil before she scribbles the order on her pad.

"Just bring it out when it's ready."

"It'll be ready at different times."

"WHEN IT'S READY!" Chucklehead grips his silverware in fists and bangs the table. The empty plates rattle against glasses of water and empty coffee saucers as the waitress walks off to bus an empty table.

"Seriously, Charles, you're bananas," I say, re-parting my hair in my reflection in the napkin dispenser.

"Charles?" Deirdre sits at a table with another man, frankly, a good-looking dude with sideburns. "Are you stalking me?" she asks.

"Oh, wow." Chucklehead's Capone *thing* generously disappears, as the Charles I know burns back into focus. "Hey, Deirdre."

"Charles, were you outside my house last night?"

"I haven't been myself lately."

"Literally," I say, sipping my espresso. So good.

"Is that why you're dressed like a gangster?" she asks. "You look ridiculous."

"Please come home." Chucklehead sounds more like Charles than ever before.

"Want to go, babe?" Sideburn touches her arm. He chews on a

toothpick.

"Who was talking to you, Sideburns?" Chucklehead gestures with his hands like a cliché.

"Don't listen to him," Sideburn says. "He's obviously cracked."

"Cracked?" Capone stirs. "I'll fucking crack you upside your fucking sideburns."

Deirdre swings her purse over her shoulder before pulling back the chair of a little boy.

"Jason." Chucklehead simmers down the Guinea. "Didn't see you there, buddy. How's my big boy?"

A fat plate of fried calamari slides onto the table in front of Chucklehead and knocks a glass of water into his lap. Water runs everywhere.

Sideburn ushers Deirdre and Jason out of the restaurant.

The waitress apologizes and brings a dish towel to soak up the water.

Chucklehead finally looks up but can't find his family. To me about the waitress, he says, "Fucking broads." He pinches a cluster of calamari into his mouth. "I need to get me a good goddamn whore." He says *whore*, but it sounds like *who-er*.

VIII.

I am playing solitaire in bed when Kitty gets home.

She says I shouldn't have waited up, something she's been saying a lot lately.

"I wanted to win one," I say, placing a two of hearts on a three of clubs. "I would have gone to bed if I had won."

"I always win when I play that game." Kitty undresses in the bathroom with the door closed and turns on the shower.

"You'll never guess what happened today." I flip through the cards in my hand one more time, before I bust. "I think Deirdre is dating a new dude."

Kitty says something and I walk to the bathroom door.

Steam fogs the room. It reminds me of a horror movie, expecting an ax to split the air as it flips end over edge into my head. I poke my head through the steam and see her clothes folded on the toilet seat.

She is on her cell phone in the shower, the water wetting her feet. Her hand traces the caulk between the white tiles on the wall. "I had fun too," she says.

IX.

We used to watch live music at a Japanese jazz club in the Kitano Hotel at 38th and Park. After the show, we'd sit on a gold bench in the lobby and wait for the doorman to hail us a cab. Kitty would rest her head at my shoulder. We don't do that anymore.

X.

I wake early the next morning to watch Kitty sleep. Didn't dream about Jeannine last night. First time in weeks. I wonder if she gave Kitty my message.

I ask Kitty if she's happy.

She snores in soft sighs.

I ask her if she still loves what we have.

She rolls away from me and says the word *holiday*.

I make coffee and bring her a cup.

"You were talking in your sleep," I say.

"You were watching me?"

"Does it matter?"

"What'd I say?"

"Holiday?"

Kitty stops blowing steam from the surface of her coffee and walks into the bathroom, locking it behind her. I crawl under the covers and whip up Jeannine. I can almost feel the stems of the maraschino cherries.

XI.

I meet Chucklehead for lunch in Brooklyn, and he tells me that he only eats pasta now. He says that DeNiro ate pasta for every meal to gain weight to play Capone in *The Untouchables*. Chucklehead orders linguini with an Alfredo mushroom cream sauce and fresh imported prosciutto.

I order the chef's salad.

Through the window, I watch a father teach his son how to ride a bicycle in the street. He holds the seat and runs behind the boy whose feet barely touch the pedals.

"Jake LaMotta in *Raging Bull*," I say.

"It was definitely *The Untouchables*."

"Six dozen of one, really."

"Whichever it was, I want to be committed like that," he says, scratching a prosthetic scar stuck to the skin, stretching from his nose to his left eye. When our food is served, he asks the waitress if his scar is on crooked. "If it's on straight, it's no good."

"Why not commit to making amends with Deirdre?" I ask.

Chucklehead lowers his face to his plate, slurping up the linguini. Alfredo sauce splashes across his cheeks. He gulps from a goblet of wine. The white napkin tucked into his shirt catches the residual splatter.

"Don't you care that you don't see your son anymore?" I stab at an egg in my salad. The hard-boiled yolk pops out of the white and hides beneath a slice of cucumber. "That you have this whole personality crisis thing going on?" I point to his scar with my fork, a piece of lettuce stuck in the prongs.

"These two clowns outside better not scratch my car." Chucklehead wipes garlic bread across his plate and rips a section off in his mouth.

"Since when do you have a car?"

The father, still trying to teach the son to ride a bike, lets go again as the boy navigates the sidewalk, the bike in a wino-wobble.

"Charles, how did you know that Deirdre was cheating on you?"

"You think Kitty is outside the marriage?"

The boy's helmet slides over his eyes.

"I don't know how to know for sure."

The handlebars cut left, driving the nose into a parked black Cadillac.

"Fucking mutt." Chucklehead stands, dropping a roll of twenties on the table. "MUTT." Chucklehead or Capone, not sure which, but definitely not Charles, approaches the father who is checking his son for injuries.

I step between them, pushing Chucklehead back, feeling a thickness in his chest. I guess the bastard really is only eating pasta.

"You call yourself a father? You," he says, wheezing. "Are dead."

"Now you're just being ridiculous," I say.

"Dad, why is that man's face so red?" the boy asks. "He looks like a red balloon."

"He thinks he's a hoodlum," the father says, moving his son to a nearby stoop before returning to Chucklehead. "Some wiseguy."

"Got something to say to me, pencil dick?"

"No one threatens my son," the father says.

"I am protecting your son. From you."

My hand now on the father's chest too, leaner than Chucklehead, I say, "Okay, Charles. Okay, sir. Let's take a minute. Just one minute. To think this out."

Chucklehead swings wide with a wild right that misses the father completely, but catches me square on the nose.

Both men watch as I stumble back like a boxer on the ropes. I tap my nostrils, but don't see any blood. My legs quake before giving out altogether. I reach for the trunk to catch myself, but misjudge and, instead, plop down into the gutter.

All I can think is, how the fuck did Chucklehead get a Cadillac?

XII.

At work I speak on the phone with a college kid about the balance on his credit card.

"You're not listening," he says. "I can't pay it."

"Not even half?"

"Not even," he says. "Not ever."

"What *can* you pay?"

"It's the reason I have the credit card in the first place, sir. To pay for shit," he says. "If I could pay with *real* money I wouldn't need the stupid thing."

"Twenty-five percent of the balance, and we'll eat the rest."

"I can't pay twenty-five cents."

"Ten percent?"

"Five."

"Sold," I say, peeking over the top of my cubicle.

Chucklehead exits the elevator with three men flanking him, each larger than the next. They walk past Chucklehead's cubicle and stop at mine. He waves the men back with a snap of his wrist, then sits on my desk. He rests his wrists on his knee and presses his finger to the phone, ending my call.

"I was negotiating," I say.

"Federal wire tap," he says. "They're all bugged," he whispers.

"He was going to pay, Charles."

"They never pay. They say they will, but they don't."

"Fan club?" I point to the men.

"Formal introductions. Parm — because he puts Parmesan cheese on everything. Killer — because he's deadly with a gun. And Tiny," Chucklehead says, straightening his necktie. "Tiny for obvious reasons." To be fair and for all practical purposes, Tiny is an elephant of a man.

"I'm not going anywhere with you or your hoods."

"This place isn't safe."

"You're not safe."

"Five minutes. All I ask. You're going to want to hear what I have to say," he says, snapping his fingers.

Coworkers peek over their cubicles as I am ushered out of the office by Capone and his enormous henchmen. They smell like Old Spice and raw meat.

Tiny, Parm, and Killer force me into the Cadillac parked outside. They burn the engine and cut out into traffic.

"Where are we going?" I ask.

"We got a rat in the house," Capone says.

"In case you haven't noticed, you're fucking nuts," I say.

"Don't be crass," he says. "It makes you sound slow."

"I can't buy what you're selling anymore," I say. "You're selling damaged goods."

"This thing of ours is only as strong as our hearts." He adjusts my shirt.

"*This thing of ours*? Is it Cosa Nostra week on A&E?"

"Your wife, Kitty, I'm sorry to say, is a rat."

"How?"

"This is an unappealing shirt on you," he says.

"Who? Who is the guy?"

"Who is your tailor? That is the real question." He snaps his fingers again at the henchmen and points to a street. "Make a right," he says. "Handmade suits. They're a thank-you from a guy I did a thing for some time back."

All five of us enter the shop, welcomed by a migraine-inducing chime.

"Charles. Tell me what you know about Kitty."

"Vincenzo," Capone says to the tailor. "My dago friend. Where are they?"

"I'm sorry, sir," a bearded man with red hair says, looking at me, then to Capone. "My name is Ronnie and, not to be rude or anything but, I have no fucking idea who you are or what the fuck you are talking about."

XIII.

At home, I call Kitty's cell.

"When will you be home?" I ask.

"Don't bother. I have dinner plans with a new client," she says. "A business man is looking to invest in some commercial real estate."

"It's not Chucklehead, is it?"

"Oh, Christ! I hate that name," she says. "Why would I eat dinner with Charles?"

"You hear about Deirdre?" I ask. "She left him."

"Can't say I blame her."

"She won't let him see Jason."

"Clean break."

"How is that clean?"

"Cut out the cancer."

"He's in rough shape. You should have seen him today. He thinks he's someone else."

"He'd be better off as someone else."

"How can you say that?"

"How can you stand that?"

"I don't understand you anymore."

"You never really have," she says.

XIV.

The next morning I walk the few blocks to Chucklehead's building. The hallway and stairs smell like takeout and ammonia. His apartment is empty of everything except for a mattress on the floor and a gutted rotary phone in the corner, its insides dangling out.

Charles stands in his kitchen wearing only his red robe, open in the front. His sides show much of the new weight he's packed on, thick rolls of fat down to his barrel-like gut. I step closer and see a divorce document, a stack of stapled papers with a yellow backer. He turns to face me, revealing the new change — a cut under his left eye, a zigzag line from his nose to his ear. Blood streaks down, but not nearly as much as I expected.

Charles says, "It's time to go to the mattresses."

XV.

Jeannine and I stare at each other while Kitty finishes up a conference call.

Jeannine wears a black pantsuit with a blue blouse and sips from a coffee mug with the photo of her three kids on it. Over their picture reads: Mom Rulz.

I keep my hands folded in my lap like a good little boy.

Kitty's door opens. She peeks out, a headset stuck over her ears, a microphone by her lips. She waves at me, then to her ear and her mouth, ending with a sharp finger to the door.

Jeannine shrugs.

Kitty says, "Egregious. Rectify this or the deal is dead."

XVI.

Chucklehead invites me over to his apartment to play cards. He wears a tuxedo and looks like a link of spicy Italian sausage. His self-inflicted wound on his face is now a scab, but with a little help will soon become a real scar. Chucklehead's sweat forms in penny-sized drops on his forehead. He has thinned out his thick black hair to reveal a balding crown.

I tell him that unlike most bald men, his hair will grow back.

Six women in black dresses drink martinis and smoke cigarettes in his living room.

"Milk Boy, walk and talk," he says, taking me into the kitchen. "I am resurrecting a once powerful and influential organization — the Brooklyn Rippers."

"You're starting a gang?"

"An organization," he says.

"Why don't you tell me what you know about my wife?"

"Not starting, so much as resurrecting." He sips espresso from a tiny cup and holds the saucer, careful not to clink.

"How far are you gonna take this Capone thing?" I ask. "Did you know Capone died of syphilis?" I point to the whores in the living room, singing along to some Sinatra song.

"I hate to be the one to do this, but I have some bad news," he says. "Your bitch of a wife is cheating on you. A fucking rat."

"What did you say?"

"I had my men check her out." He snaps, and the fat henchmen appear. "Tiny was the one to bring this matter to my attention."

"Yes. This is true. I am the one," Tiny says in a shitty Italian accent.

"Tiny, is it?" I am awash in the irony of it all. Tiny he is not. "Tell me, Tiny, what did you see, exactly."

"I saw your bitch of a wife with her foot on another man's *cacchio*."

"*Cacchio* means penis in *Italiano*," Chucklehead says, dabbing his new baldness with a handkerchief.

"You don't speak Italian," I say, waving my hands like I'm flagging down a cop.

"Something needs to be done about this," Chucklehead says. "*Capisce?*"

I point to Chucklehead's hand. "Are you seriously wearing a pinky ring?"

XVII.

Tiny tells us it's a sushi bar on the Upper East Side, but when we get there it's not. It's a Japanese jazz club — the Kitano Hotel.

A woman sings standards under a white spot of light while a man accompanies her with an expert piano. The five of us stand in the back and survey the room for my wife when Capone grabs me by the neck and points me in the direction of Kitty.

"I can't see her foot, but I bet I could tell you what it's on," he says.

Kitty and an unfamiliar man kiss over a tea light in the corner.

"Fucking whore," Tiny says.

Who-er.

"He's right," Chucklehead says. "A whore she is."

Who-er too.

It takes Kitty a moment to realize who she is looking at — me! — but when she does — *your husband!* — she says, "Fucking Jeannine told you, didn't she."

"Jeannine?" I ask.

"She told you."

"She knows?"

Even my fantasy bang has betrayed me.

The man sitting across from my wife says, "Kate, you know this clown?"

"This clown," I say, "is her husband."

"Easy, pal," he says, standing. "Let's not make this awkward."

"I'm her husband." I raise my sledgehammers, right to my face.

"Let's not make a scene."

"Kitty?" I ask.

"Kate?" he asks.

Kitty, giving up and giving over to the scene, watches the woman sing and says, "God, I used to love this place."

Her date feints a punch, before releasing a one-two combination to my chest and chin, propelling me, surprisingly, forward, settling into a sad slump at his feet.

Feet shuffle next to me as I roll out of their way.

Tiny throws a table aside, candle wax slopping to the floor. Parm and Killer control the crowd, keeping them back. The hoodlums are embroiled.

Capone walks up to the man, my wife's date, like a Roman Catholic receiving communion from a priest. Capone says, "You're a fucking rat, you know this?"

"Who are you?" he asks, looking for me on the floor.

"Before we begin," Capone says, smiling. "I want you to know something. You will not enjoy even a moment of this." Capone chokes the man with his thick hands, taking moments to slap him hard across the face. "Fucking his wife. What kind of man does that?"

The man scratches Capone, gunning for his eyes, his scab, but is unsuccessful at an escape.

Capone lifts the man, body slamming him onto a table, forcing his forearm across the man's throat like a knife lopping off his head. Their combined weight forces the table legs to snap, collapsing in a crash of bodies and broken furniture. Capone crawls on top of the man, using his new weight to pin him to the floor.

The man gags for air, his hands searching for a weapon on the hardwood floor, but only finding broken glass.

"Fucking my wife." Capone kneels on the man's chest, thumping his neck and chest and head with fat fists. "Playing father to my son. Playing house."

The man covers his head with his arms. His voice goes hoarse from the screaming.

Capone stops and stands and stomps the man with the heel of his boot. "This. Is not. Your life. You. Are not. Me."

The man goes silent and still, his arms dropping away from his face, losing the fight and control of his own faculties.

Capone, a heaving sweaty mess, steps away from a pool of urine from the man on the floor and looks into his hands splotched with another man's blood. He wipes them on his shirt. Thick red stains smear down his chest. "I need to blot this with club soda before it sets."

Police officers appear and wrestle Capone, who is at the bar blotting his shirt with a cloth napkin dipped in club soda, into handcuffs and read him his rights.

Medics hustle into the bar to attend to the man, a puddle on the floor. They do some medical tricks with smelling salts and hand-pump respirators before the man comes to again.

He thanks heaven he's alive, but feels like hell.

Capone lies on his side, his hands behind his back, suit wrinkled. His wheezing increases.

A cop says Capone has the right to an attorney. That one will be appointed for him, if he cannot afford one, which I know he can't. The cop then asks Capone if he understands his rights. I think he means Capone's parental rights, as in seeing his son, Jason.

Capone tempers his bark and before they guide him into the back of a patrol car, almost inaudibly, he says, "Please, I can't breathe."

XVIII.

In the lobby of the Kitano Hotel, I sit on a gold bench, waiting to be interviewed by the police. Kitty stands nearby, waiting to be released.

"I still love you," I say to Kitty. "Even on Sundays."

"This was the last nail in our coffin," she says.

I don't see the doorman anywhere.

XIX.

Charles sits on the stoop outside his brownstone in a tight T-shirt barely covering his gut and jeans unbuttoned at the waist. He no longer wears pinky rings, his bald spot has a thick shadow, and the scab under his eye continues to heal. He has lost some weight, noticeably in his face. His house key sits in the lock of the door below a public eviction notice posted outside.

A mattress lies in the street, parked where his Cadillac should be, an evidence bag of Al Capone's clothes on top. I kick the bag into the gutter and lift up a corner of the mattress, steering it onto the sidewalk. Charles approaches, presses his palms together on either side of the open end, and lifts with his legs.

"I'll never make it to your apartment without wheezing," he says.

"A new reality," I say.

WINTERSET SPRING

Fiction

Jonathan Liebson

The wind dropped flurries through the forest and made the fire lay flat — a full three seconds, Harold counted — while he waited for the senior patrol leader to get started. Behind him the tents ruffled angrily, the bungee cords straining to hold them in place. When the wind died down a slow hush descended over the campsite. It was here, at last, that the senior patrol leader spoke up. What they were about to hear was for present company only — no exceptions — and everyone understood he meant the scoutmaster, off running an errand at the ranger's. The words touched off an immediate excitement around the circle. On either side Harold heard whispers traded among the other Scouts, but he himself didn't participate. He'd already spent half the morning in panic, and even now he still hoped the ax might fall on someone else's head.

His worrying had begun on the bus ride to Winterset. That was when Casey had told him, in strict confidence, that the patrol leaders were planning serious payback for one of the younger Scouts. But despite all guesswork and finger pointing, Harold couldn't get him to cough up who it was — or what exactly the payback involved. It was typical of Casey. Whenever he got hold of a secret he would either talk it to death or else dangle it from the shortest leash. Eventually, Casey grew tired of Harold's pestering, so he turned to him sharply and said, "Don't worry, you'll find out soon enough!" From then on, the mystery took a dark hold of him. Halfway to Winterset he tripped over the unthinkable — that Harold himself might be the boy in question. Forget that the older Scouts barely knew who he was — that didn't stop Harold's imagination from getting carried away. Mile after mile he watched the empty farms rush by, while in his mind he fell victim to one grim scenario after another, each one allowing a slimmer margin of escape.

Presently, the senior patrol leader poked the coals with his walking stick as he looked at the circle again. He said the whole business dated back years ago, when a group of Scouts had come to Winterset to get rid of a boy they all hated. "You know the kind," he said sneering, and went on to describe a burnout that everyone in his troop, his own scoutmaster no less, wanted gone. "A bottom feeder," he declared. "A cancer to everyone. One of those kids who either pumps gas his whole life or ends up in jail."

The other patrol leaders smirked at each other while Harold, along with everyone else, turned to look at Tony Colbetti. It was undeniable — Tony fit the description to a T — and yet Harold, having now been let off the hook, was left feeling strangely, inexplicably, disappointed. He watched Tony stretch his arms behind his head and let out a big yawn, as if ready to take a nap right then. He seemed perfectly unfazed by the nasty looks being directed at him, a show of indifference Harold found completely astonishing. He wondered if anyone could really be so oblivious to that much hatred.

"So," the senior patrol leader continued, and immediately drew back everyone's attention. He explained their plan to get rid of the boy — whose name, he added, was Abel Fitch. The Scouts had planned on taking Abel on a long hike through the forest, to a hidden spring they knew of where they would all gang up and toss him in. "Everyone knew he couldn't swim," said the senior patrol leader, "so what better way to make him disappear for good?" For a moment he prodded the center coals with his walking stick before looking back up again. "It was simple enough," he said. "The boys threw him in no problem, only they didn't stick around afterward. They didn't have the *guts* — "

The senior patrol leader shook his head as if reliving the moment himself. "Of course, Abel was stubborn like they always are — so he somehow managed to dog paddle to safety. That's right — the guy didn't drown. He got away and ran tail between his legs, straight for those caves over there … "

All heads turned to follow his walking stick, which he raised toward the line of hills beyond the forest. In another second the senior patrol leader returned it to the fire. "Sure, old Abel was proud of himself — and why shouldn't he be? He'd gotten away, hadn't he? He'd outsmarted the other boys? But guess what — Abel fucked up too. He hid so deep in the caves he ended up getting lost. For a whole week he was stuck in there — remember, that's a week without sunlight, without food, without seeing another human being. A week of hearing bats fly around in the dark. Sure," the senior patrol leader went on, "Abel found his way out again, but it was too late. By then he could still hear bats in his attic."

He pointed to his head and made the sound of a cuckoo clock, triggering ripples of laughter around the circle. The senior patrol leader himself turned deadly serious, however, and told them that Abel Fitch was still known to slink around the forest at night. "I wouldn't worry about him though. Abel's too afraid of getting caught again, and with good reason. Next time he *is*," said the senior patrol leader, his head swiveling until his eyes were directly on Tony, "I can guarantee he won't get off so lucky."

In less than a second Tony had jumped to his feet. His face was bright red and he pointed a shaky finger back at the senior patrol leader, saying the story was complete bullshit. In the version *he'd* heard, the boy had gotten thrown in for dressing up like a fairy — something he said the senior patrol leader knew all about.

The other boy didn't answer him. He didn't have to — his friends started in immediately with loud cat-calls and whistling — and in no time the jeering spread like wildfire around the circle. Even the younger Scouts got involved, and Harold, shocked by the sudden turn of events, debated nervously about joining in. Tony was a head taller than him and had bullied Harold more times than he could remember, but he appeared a lot smaller suddenly, almost as if he were shrinking under the intense barrage. For several more seconds Harold carried on an anxious debate, until he noticed, just to his left, that Casey was starting to stand up. His friend winked quickly at him — offering a smug smile like he had on the bus — and that's when Harold realized what was coming. Casey had been preparing a payback of his own; he'd been waiting all along to make a showing in front of the older Scouts. A bolt of jealousy shot through Harold. A spontaneous hand, as if acting alone, pinned Casey's shoulder back down, and a second later Harold had launched himself forward instead.

What followed was something he could barely account for after the fact. A string of angry words spilled out of his mouth. *Crack-head, Burnout, Waste of Skin.* The insults came in a mad gush that was about five times louder than Harold expected it. By the time the words had run out, he discovered an entire circle of onlookers, every last one of them fallen silent. Even the wind died down again, giving way to the quiet cracking of the trees. Harold's heart switched gears suddenly, and he realized exactly what it meant to be the center of attention.

A few minutes later, as the boys came up to congratulate him, Harold wanted to explain what had really happened. He wanted to tell them it was panic — not bravery — that had made him stand his ground. Panic that had held him in place when Tony charged from across the circle. Only thanks to the senior patrol leader — who'd intervened in the nick of time — had Harold been saved. But he never succeeded in explaining himself. The compliments were dished out too quickly, the praise sank in too deep for Harold to fight it off, until at last the boys persuaded him he'd actually done something to earn their admiration. On a cloud of fame he wandered back to his tent, where another surprise was awaiting him inside. Casey yelled *"Bravo!"* as he threw Harold a hard slap on the back, and in his eyes Harold could see the boy already planning his next revenge.

The scoutmaster returned from the ranger's to give everyone a quick briefing before the afternoon hike. He didn't plan on tagging along but required each boy to partner with his tent mate. Casey, still sore from earlier, wouldn't give Harold the time of day. Harold had no problem with this — it was worth giving up Casey for the show of respect he got from the older boys. For the first time they'd welcomed him into their company, giving him random pats on the back or sending him secret looks of encouragement. He decided to let Casey pout if he wanted to. Harold himself was more than happy to move on.

The troop set out as a large group along the trail. On one side the path was flanked by a small, grassless gully, and on the other side stood the dark forest wall, which was broken up by soggy patches of snow that lay between the trees. At the head of the pack, continuing the theme from earlier, some older boys were explaining how a person could easily survive in a cave for a week. It wasn't even a question, one of them argued, as there were plenty of crickets to eat. "High in protein," he said to a friend, who winked back at him and answered, "Sure, you start with bugs, then you move up the food chain. Bats, bat shit … " Everyone but Tony started laughing.

Casey, who'd abandoned Harold for the front of the pack, launched into a story about some lost hiker in Alaska who had survived in the forest by eating ground nuts, trapping squirrels with deadfalls, and using quartz and tinder fungus to start fires. Harold wanted to laugh out loud. He couldn't believe it — almost everything Casey was saying had come straight out the Scout Handbook, yet the older boys were allowing him to go on anyway. Casey had a way of adding to the story to make it interesting — while at the same time infuriating Harold. Especially a few minutes later, when he discovered he'd gone right on listening along with the others.

After a half hour he felt a gnawing cold start in his bones. By then the group had split in two, with the younger Scouts trailing behind as they chased each other into the woods. With Casey further ahead and now basking in the spotlight, it was only Tony who paid Harold any attention. He walked with a slow, puffed-up stride, his eyes slack but somehow alert, reminding Harold of a large cat in the wild. He wasn't sure if the boy would really dare fighting him again, or worse — whether the older Scouts would come to his rescue this time. Harold decided not to risk it. The next time Tony appeared to be looking elsewhere he fell back quickly to join the younger Scouts, hoping Tony would accept this as a sign Harold had backed down.

The younger Scouts were playing the game ghost in the graveyard; as newcomer, Harold was made ghost and required to swear revenge in the name of Abel Fitch. In his first turn he caught someone easily, and as the boys regrouped, he looked ahead to notice the other party of Scouts, Tony included, putting more distance between them. He felt embarrassed all of the sudden. Of course Tony had been bluffing, the trouble had all been part of Harold's imagination. And Casey's too, he realized. He blamed his friend for having spooked him earlier, and then he blamed himself for having let Casey get inside his head

who wanted you dead. He didn't blame Abel for swimming for it. As Harold saw it, the boy had had no choice. If he got out alive, he could always seek revenge on the others, but if he succumbed to the water then the only person he'd ever end up punishing was himself.

Another hour went by. Still the river carried on in the same direction, only the banks grew wider and the water drew to a standstill, leaving only a few small eddies lathered around obtruding rocks. The sky seemed closer than before, like a dark lid drawn over the forest, while the outlines of the trees had faded into deeper shadows. Harold felt his hopelessness return; all along it had been keeping quiet pace with him, like lazy driftwood. Meanwhile, everywhere he looked his eyes and ears played tricks on him. Was he imagining it, or did the river empty into a giant opening up ahead? A sudden hole in the forest, it looked like. As he approached it he saw the clearing was rimmed with white pine trees and sycamores, and there in the middle — he couldn't believe his own eyes — a clear blue water funneling to the surface. Harold perceived the change in color before he actually understood it. While jogging toward the pool he half-expected it would disappear — like heat waves in the dead of summer — only this turned out to be no mirage. Up close he found the same mysterious blue water, a dazzling skyful in the middle of the forest. It was so exciting he almost called out at the top of his lungs. Would any of the other Scouts believe him? Of course it was the spring he'd been told about, the very same one those boys had tossed Abel Fitch into. Harold hadn't the slightest doubt in his mind. Except, as he continued staring at the water, a creeping sensation began to take hold of him. It was as if everything in the woods were also focused on the spring, like hothouse plants to a fake sun. He perceived a delicate balance around him, something he could easily shatter with the slightest misstep, and suddenly Harold recognized what was happening. He drew away quickly from the water, and from the voices urging him onward. They were the same ones he'd heard earlier today — on the school bus, at the campfire — only this time they were telling him to dive into the spring and hold his breath — and see if he could swim all the way down to the unknown bottom.

On pure adrenaline he ran almost the entire way back. Taking only a couple of short breaks along the way, he realized how slowly he'd been going earlier, how weak and spiritless he had walked. But now he felt uplifted by his secret. He'd found the legendary spring — Harold knew this like he knew what season it was — and the only thing he cared about was telling Casey. Casey would know what to do with the secret; together, the two of them could use it to their advantage.

Arriving in camp before dusk, Harold barged into his tent to find Casey relaxing on top of his sleeping bag, reading a comic book by the sallow light of a propane lantern. When Harold tried speaking with him he closed his eyes and yawned. "You're an idiot," Harold shouted, still panting from his long run — and he immediately pledged a silent treatment of his own. He felt more entitled, anyway, since if anything had happened today it would've been Casey's fault for abandoning him. But Harold soon realized, almost as quickly as he'd made it, that keeping his vow would be the hardest thing he'd ever done.

At dinner that night he nearly broke down several more times, but each time Casey signaled him to back off. Meanwhile, in small groups the younger boys discussed what precautions they would take in case Abel Fitch happened to show up. Throughout dinner the story grew in proportion, with each Scout trying to outdo the next. Someone said Abel wore a necklace of teeth from all his victims; another claimed he snacked on dried squirrel tongues like beef jerky. Overhearing, Harold couldn't tell how serious the other boys were. What they all agreed on was that, if attacked, a flashlight would be the best defense — better than a knife, even — because Abel's eyes were so sensitive to light. At that point, with the scoutmaster hovering nearby, Harold's patrol leader broke in and told them to shut up. Everyone would be fine, he said, so long as they didn't wander away from the campsite.

At bedtime, Casey nodded off almost as soon as he'd bundled into his sleeping bag. Harold felt like talking to him but knew better than to waste his breath. He zipped himself in tightly, leaving only a peephole's worth of air, and then he waited. But he couldn't say exactly what for. By then it was hard to separate everything he believed from everything he hoped was true. Trying to stay awake, he kept his hands folded over his chest and his ears wide open, but once his eyes were closed he felt his mind begin to stray outside the tent. He could hear the patrol leaders talking with the scoutmaster, their voices blending together with the sounds of the campfire and the occasional rise in wind. For now the fire would keep them safe, but Harold knew the night sky was waiting just beyond, ready to collapse on them like one big blanket of cold. Without new logs, the fire would have to go out. The coals would turn gray and dim, and soon they'd be left with only the whisper of dead flames and the rarest flicker of protection.

Asleep, Harold stumbled straight into the cold water. From the bottom he could see the sun breaking into narrow shafts on the pool's surface. A group of boys stood overlooking, waiting with rope in case he got out. He held his breath and tried swimming but the drag of water held him back. The current had turned thick and soupy, as if congealing into ice, and before long he couldn't move a single muscle. His body began sinking. From his lungs he felt the last of his air start to drain, and it was only in the final moment before death that he miraculously escaped.

The world to him had turned pitch black, soundless, and devoid of shape. Its only movement his own heart pounding rapidly in his chest. He unzipped his sleeping bag and sat up, saying, "I saw it, Casey — I swear to god I saw that pool today!" His voice sounded scratchy and distant to him. He leaned over to nudge his friend but Casey rolled away from him. "Would you shut up, you were dreaming," he said, and seemed to fall right back asleep again. In a flood of panic Harold worried the boy was right.

He was awakened the next morning by his patrol leader, who stuck his head into the tent and said, "Let's get cracking." As Harold rubbed his eyes he discovered that Casey had already left. His neck hurt from the foam bedroll and his head filled with all kinds of doubts from the previous night. Had he actually spilled his secret to Casey? And if so, would the boy run off with it and make it his own? Stepping into the campsite, Harold was grateful for the smell of breakfast and the morning air that refreshed his lungs. Even the sky had changed flags since the day before. A brand-new sun emerged above the fir trees and a flock of free-standing clouds drifted past, with large billowy caps and bearded shadows underneath.

After breakfast, three patrols set off on an all-day hike while another group went with the scoutmaster to build a footbridge over a dried-out creek near camp. The rest of the boys planned to return to the caves, and in the midst of choosing up partners Casey suddenly turned up out of nowhere. "Where have *you* been?" said Harold, but Casey held a finger to his lips as he slowly pulled Harold away from the others. He pointed over at Tony and a greasy friend of his, named Marcus. The two boys had ditched their patrols and were investigating a scrub trail into the woods. They'd tied red bandannas around their heads and were horsing about with their walking sticks.

"Let's follow them!" said Casey. His eyes were alight but he kept his voice down. "If we catch them, we can get them thrown out for good."

"Catch them at what?" Harold asked, and Casey looked at him with surprise.

"Drugs, what else?"

Of all his ideas, this was by far the stupidest. Harold thought the risk far outweighed the pay-off, and besides, he would rather go see the caves, he told Casey, since he'd missed his opportunity yesterday. What he didn't say was that by visiting the caves, he hoped — somehow — either to confirm or put to rest what his exact feelings were about the story.

"You've got all day tomorrow," Casey said. "And besides —" he was pointing his finger, "*you* need this more than anyone."

It was a snotty comment but Harold let it go. Deep down he was happy to have his friend back, and grateful Casey had chosen to include him on the adventure.

In a few minutes they set out after the other boys. Harold got into the spirit of it at first, hiding behind trees at Casey's command, squatting down military-style in the underbrush. But they kept so far back that it was hard to hear what the other boys were saying, and pretty quickly the excitement grew stale. After a mile of it Harold was ready to turn back. Not least because it had occurred to him, along the way, that even if they caught Tony and Marcus in some illicit activity, it would only be their word against the others'.

The two boys stopped walking in front of them, and Harold received a quick elbow to take cover. "My money's on hash!" Casey said excitedly. But after removing their daypacks the boys didn't produce any contraband, they only faced off with their walking sticks and began to sword fight. Their sticks made loud deflections in the forest but lagged a full second behind the action, like a movie with the sound out of sync. Tony's got knocked out of his hands and he bent down humbly to retrieve it, but on his way up he gave Marcus a surprise chop to the knees. Suddenly the sticks were dropped and the two boys were on the ground, trading positions in a wrestling match. After a few minutes it ended in a draw, with both of them lying side-by-side on their backs, huffing and puffing. Tony leaned over and put Marcus in a friendly headlock, and they both started laughing.

"I knew it," Casey whispered. "Homos!" He looked at Harold contemptuously, as if Harold himself were somehow to blame.

Sometime later, after they had fallen well out of range of Tony and Marcus, Harold started to grow anxious about something else. "You never told me about those caves," he said, trying to sound casual. "What you guys found there yesterday."

Casey was excavating a fallen tree trunk with the heel of his boot. A colony of ants bled through the tree's smashed heart, and Casey held a spit bubble on his lips before dropping it dead center. He turned to Harold slowly and looked at him for a moment, then shrugged.

"Not much proof I guess." He turned away and started walking, but Harold quickly caught up to him and demanded an explanation.

"Quiet!" Casey ordered. He cupped a hand to his ear and squinted through the trees, and in a few seconds Harold heard it too. Farther ahead, where the trail began to turn, a fast-moving stream merged alongside. It looked a lot smaller than the one from yesterday, but Harold wasn't sure. The quick glimpse he'd gotten of the trail map had indicated a number of blue lines throughout the woods, but that didn't stop Harold from all of the sudden feeling protective. Perhaps no one else had been meant to find that spring, and perhaps Harold's biggest mistake had been blabbing the news to Casey.

His friend looked at him carefully before he shrugged again.

"Like I said, not much proof. Just a pile of dead bats — a torn neckerchief. That rusty canteen could be anyone's." Bending down, he collected a fistful of pebbles that he slung into the water, pitting the surface with soft, slooshing sounds like rain. "A few of us are going back tonight," he said. "If you're up for it."

His eyes cut quickly to Harold, who in a deflated instant knew that Casey was lying. The question still remained if Harold would go anyway.

"It's okay," Casey said grinning, "you can decide later if you like." With a slap on the back he suddenly became his old self again. Running ahead, he seemed excited by every aspect of the forest, like a hound let loose after a smell. He stopped to examine the long flanks of moss running upside an ash tree, as if they might contain clues to a hidden treasure. He kneeled before some wild mushrooms with wavy orange caps like butterfly wings, and after finishing his survey he announced, "Edible." At the next patch he declared, "Non-edible," even though to Harold's eye the second group looked more or less the same.

By now the riverbanks had grown over a full body length apart, and the water looked to be a few feet deep. Without warning, Casey backed up and took a running start, and his back foot barely cleared the water on the other side. He stood perched on a small boulder in the river and stamped his heel, saying:

"This side's mine, unless you take it from me!"

He folded his arms and stomped again, but this time his foot landed funny and he lost his balance. "Watch it!" yelled Harold, but Casey's foot had already broken the plane of the water. He wheeled his arms furiously as his foot shot underneath, and Harold, even as he started toward him, knew that in a million years he would never dive in after.

Somehow Casey recovered his balance. His boot came out dark brown to the laces, his face drenched with scorn. "Why do you yell louder than a girl?" he asked. As his friend stared at him Harold very nearly laughed out loud. It was astonishing — he couldn't believe it had taken him this long — but for the first time he was finally able to see through Casey. He recognized, as the boy stood shaking away the extra drops from his boot, that Casey lived even deeper in his imagination than Harold did. So deep that he would fight tooth and nail to protect it. Well, he didn't have to worry anymore — Harold would never stand in his way again.

He'd turned and was already starting back toward camp when Casey jumped across to his side and caught him by the arm.

"Wait, take a look!"

He pulled Harold along by the coat sleeve, dragging him toward a line of paw prints backing into the woods. On hands and knees he got down and put his nose to the snow, as if picking up the scent of an animal. "I don't believe it," he said. He looked over his shoulder at Harold, shaking his head.

"What?" Harold asked. "What is it?" He watched Casey run back to the river and gather up a handful of rocks. Returning to the same spot, Casey immediately began launching them one by one in the direction the tracks led. "What do you think it is?" Harold tried again, but his friend ignored him. The stones made a terrible racket as they pounded the trees. Harold could see them ticking off branches, catching other limbs in their descent, spraying off stumps before they disappeared. Casey came back with another handful that he threw all at once, and the rocks reverberated like grapeshot throughout the woods.

But there was no report of a wild animal. All Harold heard was the heightened alarm of an unseen woodpecker, but still he kept looking. He found himself, despite how stupid it felt, simply unable to tear himself away. Here Casey must have figured him out as well. He realized that as long as he tried pulling something from the forest, Harold would be at his mercy.

"Are you crazy?" Harold shouted. "There's nothing *there!*"

Casey turned then, a strange gleam in his eyes, and he said, "Oh really?"

Two seconds later Harold heard it as well. His skin crawled, and even before looking he knew what the savage howling belonged to. He turned to see Tony and Marcus charging along the river, their heads scalped with red bandannas and their walking sticks raised high in the air like spears.

"Good luck!" Casey said, right before he bolted. Harold never even thought of doing the same. His feet went stiff and his muscles locked in place, as if every danger he'd been contemplating had turned into a straitjacket he couldn't get out of.

Next thing Tony was on him. A quick punch to the stomach doubled him over, and a jackhammer between the shoulder blades dropped him flat and face down in the snow. "You've got three seconds — " Tony said, barreling on top of him. Three seconds to apologize, he meant, for what Harold had said the day before.

Harold had every intention to. More than anything he now felt sorry for Tony, believing the boy hadn't deserved the humiliation heaped upon him. But with his breath taken away, even so few words of apology were out of Harold's reach. The count of "three" came suddenly, and with blinding speed Tony shattered a dirty snowball against Harold's face. A kick in the side after he'd jumped off — a steel toe that sent waves of pain traveling up Harold's back, and that shrugged his body like a medicine ball. It was his eyesight that now left him, and by the time it returned several seconds later, Tony and Marcus had taken off.

Harold could still hear them though. The boys had vanished but their wild cries emanated from every corner of the forest, as if instead of fleeing they were circling him in victory. He saw fat strings of saliva hanging from his lips. A shower of red dots covered the snow in front of him. Breathing again, he choked back sobs and began crawling over to the nearest tree, whose trunk became a resting place for his head. As he thought about Casey a sheet of anger burned him up. But it wasn't just Casey, it was a whole list of people who had tricked him. In his mind he began running through everyone, starting with the senior patrol leader and continuing on down, until Harold realized, with a terrible wave of shame, the person who was most responsible.

For a few minutes he simply lay there, watching as the sun cut low-angled bars through the forest. High above him the treetops had started to obscure, while in his boots he could no longer feel his toes. He was tired suddenly, in a way that had nothing to do with fatigue, and as he closed his eyes he knew he shouldn't lie around much longer, that it wouldn't be safe to. The best thing was to get up and get the blood circulating, he told himself. Yet each time he shifted he was stung by another bruise. "One more minute," he decided, but even then Harold didn't realize how far along he was. All of a sudden, like a match blown out, he was gone from the forest. He'd been kidnapped to a place unreachable by the others, hijacked to a world even he could barely believe. A world, no doubt, in which he still fought back the freezing cold, the heavy night, and the drowning water.

OCTOBER FLOWERS
Jeremy Voigt

He cans eighteen pints of tomatoes.

> She swings her legs to the floor.

He hangs vines in the back room to ripen.

> Her head swims with the dream of cow lilies.

His garden fills with the fermentation of rotting vegetables.

> She says, "I am worried," but means, "Death is near."

He feels no comfort in red pots stewing, steam collecting on eyelashes.

> She is worried; she bows to young women on the street.

He opens his chest to allow moths their escape.

> She enters without knocking, cooks a stew of petals.

He cuts off his toes to add to the tomatoes.

She pushes him to the floor; her hands bloom in his chest.

ALEX AT THE BALL GAME
Karen Schubert

My nephew Alex's wheelchair clicks
against my lawn chair legs, we rub heads,

like cats, he says. He leans
his heavy head against me. His brother's

cautious uniform is still white
in the fourth inning.

Alex flops his torso forward, studies
the grass. I bend too. We watch.

He asks for the playground, curves
his twisted fingers around the handles

of a pony on springs. His long-legged
father props him up and bounces,

giddyap, giddyap. It is hard father work.
Alex slides from every grip.

He wants to ride the swings.
No bucket seat, I am the frame

that holds legs limp as rubber bands,
my arms crisscross ribs warped like

a waterlogged boat. He wants to scrape
gravel, with my shoes I scoop a pile

for his feet to drag through.
He sees the teeter-totter,

my brother and I ride him up and down,
we're horses on the merry-go-round. He laughs.

He wants to go on the monkey bars.
His father says, *We don't know how*

those work. We return to the game
carrying buttercups, his spindle

fingers pinch the stems. The petals jostle loose.

HIDING OUT IN KETTLE FALLS
Peter Serchuk

1.
The police won't find him here.
He's carved himself into the mountain,
a face not even the weather can recognize.
All winter his footprints die in circles.
When he drives past, neighbors
wave to his ghost.

2.
In August, he comes down to buy
our peaches, not the orbs that drench
your shirt but culls you jar, three pounds
for a dollar. We talk about the orchard
and the river, what takes root
and what glides by.

3.
Rumors are ripe about his past.
Some say he's done terrible things,
others worry what he might do again.
Hypnotized by fear, most are desperate
to be his friend, to pardon the misfit
of their curiosity.

4.
The alibis are airtight, his and ours.
Nobody stands before a court of men
without his real life well hidden.
From our ladders high in the trees,
we watch his tires lift a curtain of dust
and disappear into summer.

LIFE ON PLUTO
Peter Serchuk

"Scientists decide Pluto is no longer a planet."
News headline August 24, 2006

With the papers signed
and the brutal game of what's
mine is mine resolved,
she reacquaints herself
with the world of men and
her maiden name.

At fifty-one, the sound
is not the same.
Nor the distance between
lost and found or
the landscape between
here and anywhere.

The landscape is unforgiving,
the distances scarred.
In search of bearings
she consults with friends
who direct her attention
to the self-help section.

Ignoring their advice,
she charts the evening sky
instead. Better to see herself
adrift in the spheres than
damaged or betrayed,
made invisible on Earth.

Bearings will come, she's
almost certain, if she can take
a cue from Pluto: calm in the dark,
never shamed by the sun and deaf
to those who ever named it
something more or less.

CONSOLATION
Alison Mandaville

Heath, your name like the outdoors
somewhere in England, moors,
the old land with no old growth
left. Our mother thinks of you
often, too often I think, she worries

you may have abandonment issues
like I would worry about the blue
dress I wore to Heather's wedding
more than twenty-five years ago, the elastic
not snapped, but worse, sagging,

taken one day to Goodwill. No one
will want a dress with bad elastic,
and I fear it is in the dump somewhere
in Oregon, where we grew, stretched,
moved away from. Your soon-to-be

ex-wife rails on you in emails
to our mother how you drink a quart
of gin each day, drive the kids drunk
(can I even say this out loud, while they
are still small, taut, hopeful), forget

the dinner burning on the stove, the fire
alarm just another wail in the sag
of this line. What no one can figure out
is how the alcohol skipped sideways
avoiding genetics. So it must be

because you were adopted. But I don't
think so. I think it was the genetics
of being dropped into a hole you
could never fill, the lost brother born
too broken, breathing the hospital

air just five hours in an elevator
up to the neonatal ICU, no kidneys;
do you wonder yours must work
overtime? He had an old-world name
like yours: Ian. It is no wonder

you go to the forest, get high, think maybe
you can escape gravity there, the two
lives you have been asked to live
in one. You are the one our mother
could save. My friend Heather reminded

me of you. Maybe something about
the name, the odd angle to the world
her thoughts took, her left-handedness,
and the way she played soccer as if
soccer mattered and the world could

be changed, goal by goal. I can't show
you this poem yet. I can't show our mother
this poem. I can't bring enough
concrete detail to the heart of your heart —
but if it is any consolation there are

these two things: When I was ten and waited
for the aliens to land and probably take me,
I planned who I might take along; of everyone
it was you, alive and foul-mouthed. Then too,
my little brother, look forward — at the very end,

your life, and those five hours all your own.

SHOES
Ann Walters

The cotton housedress is four sizes too big since Millie had the baby, but she wears it anyway. Her mama gave it to her as a wedding present and good thing, too, because she's got nothing else. Nothing but the dress, an old metal wash tub, and the baby.

There's that fancy apron Walter bought when he was courting her, but for some reason Millie doesn't count that. Almost a year since he started walking her home from school, talking sweet to her like she was older than twelve, older than a girl with a slingshot in her pocket and the scent of hog beneath her nails.

She doesn't count the kitchen garden, either. It might be she's not convinced about those scrawny tomatoes, cucumbers, and sweet peas.

Millie hoists the baby like an awkward thing of trouble and light and stares at the camera. The dress hangs from her like a fallen balloon, like the shreds of some other girl's flight. All she has.

Later, she'll remember more. Pines marching up the hill behind the house, a jar of honeycomb on the kitchen table. The baby, the too-big dress, and on her feet, shoes.

IMPRESSIONS

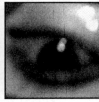

False Shadows
Rob Shore

Nighttime Glow
Amanda Gahler

Light, Dark, and Leaves
Amanda Gahler

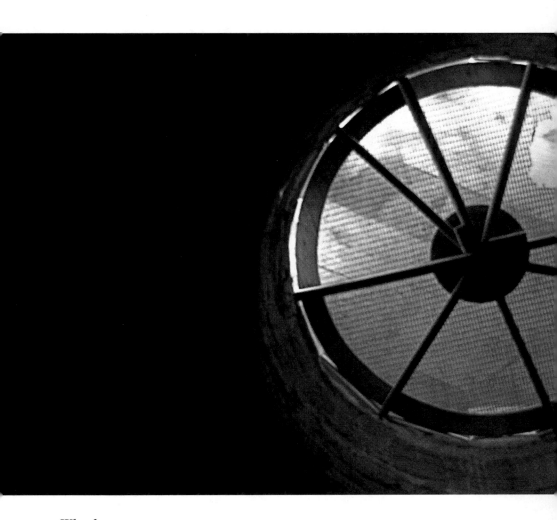

Wheel
Rob Shore

Twisted
Maxwell Teitel-Paule

Music Waiting to Happen
Amanda Gahler

Noon Nap
Petra Ford

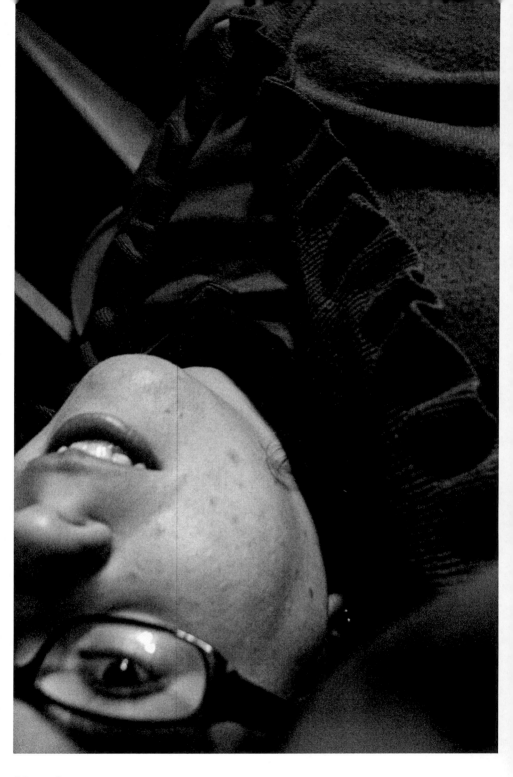

Monocle
Rob Shore

Enter
Kristen Spickard

Mail at Jenner
Maxwell Teitel-Paule

Smokey
Thomas Krapausky

Emelyn Story
Maxwell Teitel-Paule

Due
Kristen Spickard

AMERICA'S LAST NATURAL MAN: *Nonfiction*
THE STORY OF ISHI
Stephen Thomas

Emergence. This story starts near a slaughterhouse in the late afternoon, on August 28, 1911, in Oroville, California. Oroville (*gold town*) is on the east side of the Sacramento Valley about one hundred fifty miles northeast of San Francisco. Workers leaving the slaughterhouse in near one hundred degree heat happened upon a man, barefoot, dressed in rags crouched in brush, near starvation. He was immediately suspected of thievery. He offered no resistance to the workers. They called the local sheriff who took the man into custody and placed him in the Oroville jail. The captive uttered a few words, but nothing which could be understood by anyone present. The *Oroville Register* reported the following day:

An aboriginal Indian, clad in a rough canvas shirt ... was taken into custody last evening by Sheriff Webber. ... In the sheriff's office he made a pathetic figure crouched upon the floor. He is evidently about 60 years of age. ... Over his shoulder a rough canvas bag was carried. In it a few manzanita berries were found and some sinews of deer meat. By motions, the Indian explained that he had been eating these. ... Apparently the Indian has never come in contact with civilization, except as he has assisted in robbing some lonely cabin near his hiding places.

... The attire of the Indian, his general appearance and his presence here, are strongly indicative of the fact that he belongs to the Deer Creek tribe of wild and uncivilized Indians. These Indians were originally proud and warlike, and their frequent depredations upon the white settlers led to an organized war against them. ... Two years ago a surveying party drove the Indians from their last hiding place. As far as could be ascertained, the remnant of the once proud tribe at that time consisted of four bucks and one squaw. ... It is believed that the aborigine who was captured last evening is either the last surviving member of the party, or that he was the one delegated by the others to make a foray upon the slaughterhouse.

While in custody, the man was given food, as curious townspeople looked on. He looked back at his onlookers, not showing fear and taking a lively interest in the strange food given to him, including bread and butter, a doughnut, an orange, a banana, a tomato. He showed obvious distaste with the banana until he was shown that it must be peeled before it is eaten. On the strength of this learning, he proceeded to try similarly to peel the tomato. On August 30 the *Oroville Register* reported:

... the Indian found on Monday yesterday told [in the weird pantomime, which has in all ages been the medium through which people of different tongues converse] the story of his wanderings. The tale more firmly confirms the belief that the Indian is the last surviving member of the uncivilized Deer Creek Indians. ... All day long there was a continual stream of people passing upstairs to the cell in which the Indian was kept. It is estimated that there were fully 1,000 people who viewed the Indian yesterday.

The Oroville authorities were in a quandary. The man in their custody could not be charged with any crime. He was not hostile in any aspect of his behavior. He showed no interest in being returned to the hills from which he had come. He did not react in any way to suggest that he was even distantly related to any of the other Native Americans in the area who were brought to see him. The Oroville authorities then received an urgent telegram from A. L. Kroeber in San Francisco, as follows:

Sheriff Butte County. Newspapers report capture wild Indian speaking language other tribes totally unable to understand. Please confirm or deny by collect telegram and if story correct hold Indian till arrival Professor State University who will take charge and be responsible for him. Matter important account aboriginal history.

Alfred L. Kroeber sent this wire in his capacity as the chair of the new Department of Anthropology at the University of California, Berkeley. Kroeber, born in New Jersey in 1876 received a Ph.D. in anthropology (only the second such degree awarded in the United States) in 1901 from Columbia University where he was a protégé of Franz Boas, founder of modern anthropology in the U.S. Boas believed in *fieldwork* rather than the anecdotal, armchair, "my travels among the aborigines of (wherever) ..." kind of anthropology fashionable among the Victorians. Kroeber soon settled on a position in the new department of anthropological studies at Berkeley, passing up overtures from Chicago's Field Museum of Natural History. His special interests were the language and culture of indigenous tribal communities, particularly those in California and Mexico. But Kroeber was a true generalist, equally at home in linguistics, archaeology, and cultural studies. He soon became a giant in his field, remaining so until his death in 1960. He served as department head at Berkeley for more than forty years and wrote more than five hundred books and articles. What's more, he looked the part of the serious scholar and was much emulated for two generations.

Back to Kroeber's telegram. He and the Oroville authorities soon received approval from the U.S. Bureau of Indian Affairs in Washington to bring the *wild Indian* to San Francisco. Kroeber sent Tom Waterman, another former anthropology student of Columbia's Franz Boas, whom

Kroeber had hired in 1907 in his growing department. Waterman had done exploratory work to no avail in 1908 in the Oroville area, looking for evidence of elusive, remnant Native American people. A small group, including an elderly woman, had been stumbled upon in hiding in a remote canyon cave by a surveying party earlier that year.

Waterman came to Oroville by train and tried to communicate with the captive using vocabulary lists he and Kroeber thought might be helpful. There was no success until Waterman tried the word in the Yana language for yellow pine — *siwini*. Instant success, as the man's eyes lit up and he repeated the word, tapping on his wooden cot, *siwini, siwini*. It soon became clear that this man (he was soon to be named *Ishi*, the word in his language for "man") was a Yahi. The Yahi were a tribelet from the southernmost range of a small tribal group known as the Yana. They had lived, possibly for several thousand continuous years, in the westward facing foothills of the Sierra Nevada mountain range along the fringe of the east side of the northern Sacramento Valley.

There had been limited contact between the elusive Yana and the Spanish and other early ranchers in the valley, but the end of these people came with the gold miners of 1849. By 1865 only a small southernmost remnant of the Yana were left in their presettlement range. In simple terms, it was a genocide, not accidental, not well-organized, not mandated by any public authority, but deliberate and effective. Here are some numbers from a 1906 congressional report to the Bureau of Indian affairs: There were about two hundred sixty thousand Indians in California in the early 1800s. This number was reduced, primarily in the 1850s, and mostly by some two hundred thousand miners, by more than ninety percent The known remainder, just above seventeen thousand were by 1906 scattered among the general population or on a few reservations. This was mainly because the new people, the *saldi*, the white men, had fire sticks that could make holes in the bodies of the Yana people. There was no chance for coexistence when the miners started work in the caves and streams which the Yana had used for many centuries. One of my sources states that the California Gold Rush resulted in the largest human migration since the Crusades. Ishi was born during this era, perhaps as late as 1860. When he was found in Oroville, he was the last Yahi alive, having survived essentially as a fugitive for his entire life, the last two or three years alone. The dying woman the surveyors had found in the cave in 1908 was Ishi's mother.

Waterman returned to San Francisco by train with Ishi on September 4, having excitedly written to Kroeber just before leaving Oroville:

He recognizes most of my Yana words ... I get a few endings that don't occur in Northern Yana ... he has some of the prettiest cracked consonants I have ever heard. ... He will be a splendid informant.

From Ishi's perspective, it had been a big week. He had emerged from a life of isolation, possibly unintentionally as a result of exhaustion and hunger. He had every reason to expect to be killed by the *saldi* who captured him. Strangely, they had not harmed him and had fed and clothed him. Now he was being taken away by a *saldi* who could speak some of his language on a smoking, whistling, serpent-like demon which from his vantage point in the hills had seemed to gobble up all the *saldi* which it managed to pull through its skin so as to devour them inside.

What's the connection here? Someone asked me as I was telling them about preparing this paper: "Of all the thousands of subjects to write about, why are you writing about this California Indian who has been dead for many decades?"

Here's my answer: My father was born in Kentucky in 1907. His ancestry has been traced back no further than to his grandparents, although he told me he thought he might be related to a "Thomas" who came through the Cumberland Gap with the Daniel Boone group in the 1770s. I cannot verify this. My grandmother, Anna Susan Osborne, born in 1879, was a twin. A grandson of her twin sister once told me that he was convinced, upon seeing his grandmother after she had died in the late 1950s, he was looking at a Cherokee woman. The same conclusion can be drawn from pictures of my grandmother in her later years. Thus, it is at least plausible to me that there is some Cherokee or other Indian ancestry in my paternal line. The records are very sparse when it comes to frontier communities in the eighteenth and early nineteenth centuries in Kentucky. There was frequent cohabitation or contact involving settler men and local Indian women. The primary reasons for this were that women were reluctant to move away from older and safer communities in the East to the dangerous conditions on the frontier, and mortality of women on the frontier was high, particularly during and after childbirth. So there was a chronic shortage of women west of the Atlantic states and, thus, the inevitable attraction of frontiersmen to Native American women.

My father's family came north from a backwoods farm in Hodgenville, Kentucky, (birthplace of Abraham Lincoln) to Bloomington, Illinois, around 1915. My father was then seven or eight years old. World War I and the 1920s provided good employment opportunities to his father and older brothers in the upper Midwest. But by the early 1930s my father (one of eleven children most still at home in these Great Depression years) elected not to finish high school and to travel west on freight trains with friends, spending three or four years knocking about doing ranch work, odd jobs, later joining CCC and WPA work projects. He went through Colorado and Wyoming on these travels, eventually through California from north to south, and finally through Arizona and Texas coming back to the Midwest sometime after 1935. It was his "grand tour," and he had many stories about this period which he told over the years. I wish I had paid greater attention to them.

In the early 1970s, visiting my parents at their home in Peoria, Illinois, I came upon a book about Ishi which was a discard from the local library where my father was a board member. This book was mostly pictures and intended for young readers. I clearly remember being impressed both with the story and the photographs. By that time I had been back several years from service in the early 1960s with the Peace Corps in Africa where I lived for more than two years in close contact with indigenous people (my own "grand tour"). I have no recollection of talking about Ishi with my father, but he had a great interest in the prehistory of North and South America, and I am sure that is how the Ishi book came to our house.

Now push the fast forward button and move up about thirty years to the present. I am a student in the M.L.A. [Master's in Liberal Arts] degree program at the University of Chicago. In the early 2006 term, I took a course with Professor Bertram Cohler which had an extensive reading list in later nineteenth and early twentieth century sociology, anthropology, and psychology (Karl Marx, Max Weber, Emile Durkheim, Claude Levi-Strauss, Sigmund Freud and others). One of the books assigned was *Tristes Tropiques* (1955) by Claude Levi-Strauss. This superb French scholar was born in 1908 and is still alive today. He is the originator of what has come to be termed the school of "structural anthropology," broadly meaning that what is important about *things* is their relationship to other *things* rather than the *things* themselves. Thus, communities and people are studied according to their social structure, particularly in relation to structural opposites such as young / old, women / men, married / unmarried, high status / low status, acceptable / unacceptable behavior, and so on. *Tristes Tropiques* is partly autobiographical and partly a kind of thinking man's travelogue concerned with Levi-Strauss' work in central South America in the 1930s and 1940s. He has refused to sanction any English language rendering of the title of his 1955 book because of the special affective quality of the title in French which connotes a sadness for what is gone, never to be replaced, having been destroyed mostly by deliberate or inadvertent contact with the external world. *Tristes Tropiques* is literally *sad tropics*, but the connotation is deeper than that. As I was reading this book, I came upon the following passage:

It must have been an extraordinary advantage to have access to communities which had never yet been the object of serious investigation and which were still quite well preserved, since their destruction had only just begun. Let me quote an anecdote to illustrate what I mean. An Indian, through some miracle, was the sole survivor after the massacre of certain savage Californian tribes. For years he lived unnoticed in the vicinity of large towns, still chipping stones for the arrow-heads with which he did his hunting. Gradually, however, all the animals disappeared. One day the Indian was found naked and dying of hunger on the outskirts of a suburb. He ended his days peacefully as a porter at the University of California.

I immediately wrote in the margin — *ISHI! Why didn't he use his name?* I had no recollection of hearing or seeing anything about Ishi during the preceding thirty years since my encounter at home with the Ishi book back in the 1970s, but the name came immediately to mind. I did some checking and soon learned that no biography of Ishi existed prior to Theodora Kroeber's well-received work, *Ishi in Two Worlds*, published in 1961. Thus, Levi-Strauss, writing in 1955, may have recalled some reference to this man in the professional literature of his day, but there is no reason he would have ever seen or heard the name *Ishi*, the name assigned to him by his keepers at the California museum.

That is the background to my renewed interest in Ishi. A few weeks ago, I was traveling with a naturalist group in the Hopi / Navajo country of northeastern Arizona. We were at the home of Ruby Chimerica, a Hopi weaver, storyteller, community leader and ambassador, who was speaking to us of the fragility of Hopi culture. The Hopi language and much of the culture are well documented, and the Hopi dance tradition is alive and well. But for decades English has been the language of the schools. Many Hopi adults know little of the Hopi language, speaking English even at home. There are about fifteen thousand people listed in the present Hopi tribal register. Are they enough to insure the long-term survival of the spoken Hopi language? Probably not. By contrast, there are more than two hundred thousand Navajos, and their cultural preference is to have as little contact with *Anglos* as possible. Thus, the very complex Navajo language has better prospects of long-term survival than the Hopi language at present. Now, back to Ishi, the last speaker of the Yahi variant of his Yana language. Before European contact there were as many as one thousand such languages in North America. *Tristes pour Nord Amerique.*

Fortuitous timing. In the fall of 1911, Kroeber was about to open a new departmental museum in San Francisco in a former law school facility on Parnassus Heights next to the medical school looking over Golden Gate Park toward the ocean. The university had acquired this property in 1903 mainly to store the collection of donor Phoebe Apperson Hearst, an avid collector of art objects and archaeological materials. Her husband had been a wealthy mine owner; her son was William Randolph Hearst, the newspaper tycoon. Caretakers regularly lived in the museum to see to its security and that of its collections. These living quarters were not elaborate but comfortable and sufficient. Ishi was brought to the museum, met Kroeber for the first time, and soon settled in to its living space. The press and the public were demanding information about him, especially his name and that of his tribe. After all, every Indian has a name and a tribe, such as *Little Beaver from the Blackfeet* and the like. Ishi's real name, what he was called by his own people, will never be known. It is not clear that he ever shared his tribal name with anyone, as it would be a cultural taboo for him to tell his name to strangers. Thus, *Ishi — man*. And for his tribe — *Yahi*, his word for his *People*, rather than the more prosaic, a member of the *Mill Creek Group* or a *Southern Yana*.

The museum which was now his home opened to the public a few weeks after Ishi's arrival in San Francisco by train, then ferry and streetcar. Thousands came on Sunday afternoons to see Ishi, seated with Kroeber, demonstrating the arts of his people, making arrowheads and spear points, bows and arrows, imitating the calls of animals and making fire with little more than his bare hands and a wooden fire drill. Ishi soon learned enough English words and city customs to move freely about the museum, its grounds and surrounding city streets. His cheerful demeanor produced many casual friendships. He was a frequent guest at the homes of museum staff and departmental faculty, including that of chairman Kroeber. Over time, his only regular duties consisted of the Sunday afternoon sessions with the public and part-time work in the museum as a janitorial assistant. He was paid twenty-five dollars a month from museum funds. He loved to be with children, and they with him.

Ishi was in contact with other Indians in San Francisco, especially an elderly mixed Yana / Maidu gentleman from an area north of Ishi's Yahi country. This was Sam Batwi who knew enough both of English and Ishi's language to serve as a communications bridge in the early days. Ishi did not like Sam, a bearded, wire-spectacled, fancy-dressed, know-it-all, and generally condescending person who looked upon Ishi as a hapless bumpkin from the woods.

We have spoken of the three most important people in Ishi's post-emergence life, Kroeber, Waterman, and Batwi. To these three, Saxton Pope ("Popey" to Ishi) should be added. Pope was a surgeon who was Kroeber's age and taught at the medical school adjacent to the museum. Pope examined Ishi early on and became his doctor. Pope soon became fascinated with Ishi's archery skills and Ishi with Pope's sleight-of-hand tricks. It is fair to say they became soul brothers, spending much time together. Ishi's entire method of handling his bow and arrow (how he stood or crouched, the placement of his hands on the bow, string and arrow, and the manner of release) is found nowhere else in Native American culture, but is found in Mongolian or Asiatic practice. This lends credence to the suggestion that Ishi's people were directly descended from Asian ancestors and that this aspect of their culture had remained unaffected by contact with other groups of Native Americans through several millennia.

As time progressed, one of Ishi's favorite pastimes was to wander the halls of the hospital, visiting patient rooms, chatting amiably in broken English and Yahi with persons who were often very ill. These patients, as well as hospital staff, generally welcomed his visits. In all the reading I have done, while I have found references to Ishi being startled, confused, and even repulsed by the strange ways of the *saldi*, he always remains cheerful and never expresses resentment or anger. No wonder he survives to this day as a beloved figure by those who feel they have come to know him.

The United States Bureau of Indian Affairs had taken no interest in Ishi or his people prior to his emergence. But two months after the bureau had approved his removal from the Oroville jail to the care of Kroeber and Waterman, the bureau wrote their agent in California:

It is difficult to form a clear idea as to the possibilities in this Indian as regards civilization ... As this Indian has been in the care of the authorities (at the museum) for some time, they have had opportunity to make observations and to gain some idea of his intelligence, and capacity for civilization. Make inquiry with special reference, first, to the possibility of training him to conform, at least to a reasonable degree, to the customs of civilized life; and, second, as to the possibility of training him for the performance of simple manual labor.

Kroeber, understandably incensed when he read this directive, replied succinctly and directly, as follows:

I beg to state that from the outset Ishi has conformed very willingly and to the full extent of his understanding, to the customs of civilized life.

There was further correspondence with the bureau in 1914 in which they observed that Ishi's mental development, according to the opinion they had received, *was not beyond that of a six-year-old child.* Kroeber again replied, confirming that Ishi was doing well and preferred *his present condition* to a permanent return to his old home. The bureau record ends there.

Inevitably, the time came to consider a return visit with Ishi to his homeland. It took Kroeber and Waterman some time to persuade Ishi to make this excursion. He had several objections: 1. There were no beds, chairs, or tables around his Mill Creek ancestral home. 2. It could be cold, wet or both, and there were no roads or trails. 3. There was very little to eat in this place.

Ishi may also have had some residual fear of being abandoned in the land of the dead, left alone among his murdered people. Many had never been given proper funeral rites according to their custom. But Kroeber and Waterman were insistent, and Dr. Pope was anxious to join, along with his eleven–year-old son whom Ishi knew well. Off they went to Deer and Mill Creek country in early May, 1914 spending a month with Ishi, visiting the hunting grounds, fishing streams, and places where he had resided in his more than fifty continuous years. The Yahi followed the seasons spending spring and early summer close to the lush new growth in the Sacramento Valley, moving up in the foothills as the summer weather heated lower elevations, being always mindful of the need to store nonperishable food (seeds, acorns, nuts, dried fish, and meat) in secure areas to be consumed during the cold winter months. Ishi demonstrated to the party the full range of his survival techniques.

I love to camp and spend as many nights outside each year as possible from spring well into the fall. It takes work to live outdoors even if you don't have to find your own food, make your own clothes, baskets, and tools or look for firewood. In Ishi's case, it was also necessary to be mindful of the fact that you would be hunted down and killed if you let strangers or their dogs become aware of your presence through the slightest sound, scent, footprint, wisp of smoke, or other sign.

The expedition was a great success. Much was learned for the anthropological record, and Ishi enjoyed being safe in his old home territory in the company of his new friends. One of the few times of distress to Ishi occurred when one of the party killed and brought to camp a rattlesnake, insisting that it be cooked and eaten. Ishi would have no part of this. These snakes were to be avoided, and never handled in a way disrespectful to their life which could unleash their power to do evil. Ishi was surprised that the party survived this incident. They happily retuned to San Francisco on June 1, 1914.

Death in a museum. Ishi developed a troubling cough in December, 1914. During January, 1915 he was checked by Dr. Pope and others in the hospital next to the museum. Tuberculosis was suspected but could not be confirmed. By late spring, he had bounced back and spent the summer with the Watermans where a linguist worked extensively with Ishi each day, recording all he could of the Yahi language. Ishi weakened again at the end of the summer and came back to the museum in September to be closer to Dr. Pope ("Popey").

Through the balance of 1914 and into 1915, Ishi was gravely ill with tuberculosis. Meanwhile, thousands were dying almost daily on the battlefields of Europe and a great influenza epidemic was about to begin which would take several million lives. Kroeber was in the east and in Europe on a one-year sabbatical but kept in close touch regarding Ishi's condition. Ishi spent time in the hospital but near the end was relocated to a room in the museum where an exhibit was dismantled so that he could have lots of sunlight and a view of the nearby park. Kroeber and Gifford, the museum director, corresponded as to funeral details as the situation worsened. Ishi died on March 25, 1916. Kroeber had written to Gifford on March 24, in a letter not received until just after Ishi's funeral:

Please stand by our contingently made outline of action, and insist on it as my personal wish. There is no objection of a cast (death mask). I do not, however, see that an autopsy would lead to anything of consequence ... Please shut down on it. As to disposal of the body, I must ask you as my personal representative to yield nothing at all under any circumstances. If there is any talk about the interests of science, say for me that science can go to hell.

Ishi's remains were cremated and placed in a Pueblo Indian jar in Niche 601 at Mount Olivet Cemetery south of San Francisco, near to what was until recently, but not then, called Candlestick Park. A handful of people attended the funeral, including Waterman, Pope, and Gifford who reported the basic details to Kroeber in a letter dated March 30:

The only departures from your request were that a simple autopsy was performed and that the brain was preserved. The matter was not entirely in my hands — in short what happened amounts to a compromise between science and sentiment with myself on the side of sentiment. ... [Ishi] told Pope sometime ago that the way to dispose of the dead was to burn them, so we undoubtedly followed his wishes in that matter. In the coffin were placed one of his bows, five arrows, a basket of acorn meal, ten pieces of dentalium, a boxful of shell bead money ... a purse full of tobacco, three rings ... all of which we felt sure would be in accord with Ishi's wishes. ... The inscription of the jar reads ISHI, THE LAST YANA INDIAN, 1916.

The rest of the story. Ishi's death and burial were noted in the press as he had achieved fairly widespread notoriety as the *wild Indian who lived in a museum.* Then the screen went blank. For nearly fifty years, essentially nothing was said or written about Ishi. Virtually nothing by Kroeber or by Waterman or Gifford or anyone else who had known Ishi personally. Why? I mentioned earlier how I backed into the probable reason for the oblique reference to Ishi in 1955 by Claude Levi-Strauss. I went to the web and started gathering some information. Most of it started with references to Theodora Kroeber's *ISHI in Two Worlds* published in 1961. More than a million copies have been printed. It was a best-seller, translated into several languages, and excerpted in *Reader's Digest.* Theodora Kroeber's book led in many ways to Ishi's rebirth, just as the work of another scholar, Orin Starn, we shall soon learn, led to the reburial in his home territory of Ishi's entire physical remains, not just those placed in Niche 601.

We have to return to Alfred Kroeber. In 1913 Kroeber's first wife, the beautiful and charming Henriette Rothschild, died of tuberculosis at the age of thirty-six. Then Ishi died in 1916. Kroeber at age thirty-nine was much shaken by these events. He was not well himself, suffering from what he would learn was Meunier's disease which led to his deafness in one ear. He was exhausted from fourteen years of work on his nine hundred ninety-five page *Handbook of the Indians of California* which was published in the 1920s and remains influential today. He later termed the time from 1915 to 1922 his *hegira*, a kind of exodus episode. He entered psychoanalysis and in due course qualified and practiced for a time as a lay analyst. He did not sever ties with the university in Berkeley or with anthropology. He pressed on and muddled through.

Now I turn to Theodora Kracaw, as she was known before she met and married Alfred Kroeber. Theodora was born in 1897. Her mother had been raised by a pioneer family on a Wyoming ranch. Theodora grew up in the west, spending her first eighteen years in the gold and silver mining town of Telluride, Colorado, riding her Navajo-trained pony. Her early years were spent in close connection with the culture and company of native Americans in Colorado. As a Berkeley student in 1918, she took a class with Alfred Kroeber. Then in 1919, she married a frail San Francisco lawyer who died in 1923 leaving Theodora, at age twenty-six, with two small children. In 1925, she reconnected with Kroeber (twenty years her senior) at a reception for Margaret Mead. They were soon married, and by the end of the 1920s had two more children of their own.

Theodora and others occasionally pressed Alfred to do something to preserve Ishi's story to which he always demurred. I think it was grounded in his aversion to the anecdotal school of anthropology and to the dangers of generalizing from a sample of one. He was an academic, not a storyteller. There may also have been deeper issues in which he found it difficult in retrospect to decide whether he had done the right thing in bringing Ishi to San Francisco. In the late 1950s, by which time Kroeber was well into his seventies, Theodora took up this project herself, with the spectacular results noted above. She singlehandedly resurrected Ishi or at least his story.

Theodora was a sensitive and skilled writer, but not a professional historian and neither a scholar nor an academic. She had the help and encouragement of one of Kroeber's successors at Berkeley, Robert Heizer, full access to the archival records at Berkeley and the museum, and daily access to her husband, one of the few people then living who had known Ishi. Was her book, therefore, complete and accurate?

It is commonplace to say that those who turn raw historical events into a contemporary narrative often leave their own fingerprints on the account they produce. I will not judge Theodora negatively. Without her, this story would not have been told. She may have guarded her husband's reputation with great care. She may have romanticized Ishi as emblematic of a healing process among diverse elements of American society which was emerging in the late 1950s and is still a work in progress today. She may have occasionally failed to dig deeper into areas of the record which did not suit her ends. So what? She remains the *sine qua non* of this story.

Orin Starn is a professor of cultural anthropology at Duke University. He grew up in an academic family in Berkeley in the 1960s and 1970s, dropped out of college for a time in the early 1980s, spent some time on the Navajo reservation and returned to college at the University of Chicago, studying anthropology. In the late 1990s Starn decided to take a fresh look at the Ishi story, it being almost forty years since Theodora Kroeber's book was published. Starn refers to Ishi as one of his childhood heroes. The result, some seven years later, is Starn's engagingly written book, *Ishi's Brain* (2004). Three word summary: Times have changed. It is a kind of academic version of CSI (the popular TV series concerning crime scene investigations).

Here is a brief outline of Starn's perceptive detective work and the outcome: Recall Kroeber's mandate that there be no autopsy of Ishi — *science can go to hell.* An autopsy was performed. Starn found the report. Ishi's brain was removed and preserved, and according to second- or third-hand oral reports which reached Starn, sent off to the Smithsonian where it had later been destroyed. Berkeley said, *Not true.* The Smithsonian said, *Not true.* Starn pressed on until he found this note to Kroeber dated December 30, 1916 in a bundle of papers in the Berkeley archives: ... *the National Museum will be very glad to receive the brain of Ishi which you offer to present* ... Starn soon found a letter to the Smithsonian written by Kroeber on October 27 of that year: *I find that at Ishi's death last spring his brain was removed and preserved. There is no one here who can put it to scientific use. If you wish it, I shall be glad to deposit it in the National Museum collection.*

Starn confronted the Smithsonian with this record. At length, the museum acknowledged that the brain had been placed there. Starn had headed down this trail in part because Art Angle, a Native American activist from Ishi's general area, had become aware of the Ishi story and believed his remains should be returned to the ancestral grounds under the Native American Graves Protection and Restoration Act of 1989.

After a lengthy, legally complex and contentious process, Ishi's entire remains were united and returned to his homeland. They were placed in a basket and buried in the ground near Deer Creek sometime late in 1999. This was not a public event. There is no marker. Those few present took an oath of secrecy.

Endnote. In April, 1962, Fred H. Zumwalt Jr. wrote to Theodora Kroeber thanking her for *Ishi in Two Worlds* and recalling in vivid detail many happy hours he spent with Ishi during Zumwalt's childhood in San Francisco. Here is a brief excerpt including a real global village scene from his letter of April 24:

My name was difficult for him so that he gave me the name of MUT ... His name for our Chinese laundry man was "Kite" after "Kite" brought me a dragon-kite, dried lichee nuts, ginger, and brown sugar sticks on Chinese New Year in 1915. Ishi loved the sugar sticks and the Kite but not the lichee and ginger. Kite showed Ishi how to fly the kite and we must have been a sight to watch, the Chinese with black baggy pants, wearing a que, a black skull cap and felt slippers, Ishi in a scotch plaid wool shirt, but barefoot and I in a sailor suit. ... It is said "no person is truly dead until no one left on earth has any recollection of that person" so Ishi lives again brought back to life by your efforts.

NOM DE GUERRE   *Fiction*
Joel Fishbane

The two soldiers left at the start of the war, and because they lived next door, they wrote to their wives on the backs of each other's letters. This was both a convenience and a necessity, since paper was precious and both men had a limited vocabulary. It takes a poet to describe a war, but the first man was a fisherman, and the second made hats, and neither quite knew a lyrical way to tell his wife what was truly happening all around him.

At first, there was some confusion. Both women were called Marie, while both men were called Jean, a situation which might have been odd in any place other than Quebec where such names are as common as the wind. To make matters worse, the family name was also identical, a result of some distant blood tie no one could ever ascertain. With no choice but to read both sides of the page, the women became privy to the greatest secrets of each other's lives. As may be expected, this was a dangerous pastime. The first Marie envied the second Jean's way with words, while the other Marie become jealous of the first Jean's passion. When the men received their own letters, written separately, they found the sentences terse, the paragraphs filled with tension, and they quickly realized they would have to come up with a better plan.

It was in this way that the fisherman's wife became mon petit flétan while the other Marie came to be called mon gros chapeau. The men did not warn their wives in advance, yet when the mail came, each woman knew instantly which side of the page was for her. For almost a year all confusion abated, and whenever the postman arrived with letters from the front, there was always one addressed in that memorable way: Á mon petit flétan et mon gros chapeau: To my little halibut and my enormous hat.

Mon petit flétan was a small, wispy thing with a soft, white belly and hair of blackish-gray. She was adept at all manner of things, such as needlework and baking, but what made her extraordinary was her ability to gut a fish faster than anyone else in town. Her reputation extended so far that it was normal for someone to wander in from the outside world, planning to make a name for themselves. Mon petit flétan found the whole thing rather foolish, but she was a good sport, and one year agreed to gut fish for charity during which for a whole day people donated a dime for every fish she dismantled.

She was twenty when she was caught by the fisherman. Her talents had helped her find work at the *poissonnerie*, and the first time she met her Jean, she had been wearing a smock splattered with innards.

Yet, such was her beauty that he loved her anyway. Their courtship adhered perfectly to the morality of the age, which meant they had sex before marriage but did not discuss it. She had a womb begging to be filled — after the war, she would have six children in five years — but it also seemed to have an intelligence all its own. It rejected every offering that came before V-Day, as if it knew to do otherwise would only create trouble.

The fisherman was not the only one who loved her, and after he left, she remained a popular object of affection. For two years in a row, she was crowned carnival queen, a feat so rare for a married woman that many supposed she must still be a virgin. A rumor began that her marriage had never been consummated; one so eagerly believed that those devoted to conquering her convinced the priest to suggest annulment. The priest did his duty, only to have mon petit flétan reply that even if it was true her marriage had not been consummated, which it wasn't, she would still remain loyal to her husband, for that was the very definition of love.

At this her suitors only laughed. The war may last forever, they said, but she won't. They remained optimistic, and the little halibut had no choice but to spread the word that even if the fisherman were killed in combat, she highly doubted she would ever marry again.

Mon gros chapeau loathed her name. Wound as tight as a hat cord, she was like a used turban: creased and on the wrong side of being in style. She was widowed when she met the milliner. Her first husband was a terrible man, both impotent and cruel; when he was taken by typhoid, she deemed it a fortunate thing, for it saved her the trouble of deciding which was more scandalous, murder or divorce. A year and a day after he was buried, she went to buy a new hat, and the milliner had only to wrap the measuring tape around her head for the two to know they were in love.

They married quickly, for she was pregnant, a secret only the milliner knew on the day he left for war. By the time he christened her "mon gros chapeau," he believed the baby was in its seventh month. It was an understandable, if unfortunate, mistake: His wife had not yet told him she had suffered a miscarriage weeks before. War is full of grief, she thought. I don't have the heart to tell him that senseless death is happening here, too. Secretly, though, she harbored the fear that her pregnancy had been the sole reason for their marriage. Her cynicism would never let her believe in true love, and her ego would never let her admit that it could happen to her.

The miscarriage had happened early enough so that few knew she had been carrying. Had he known, the gossipy postman might have exercised unique caution, but instead he told everyone he knew. The new name spread like a plague. Before long, everyone was calling her "mon gros chapeau," creating a neurosis which dogged her the rest of her life. She was content as long as there was nothing *gros* about her, but if she thought for a moment she might actually deserve the name, she would spiral into brief fits of anorexia. She ran the millinery in her husband's absence, and it became common for someone to come looking for a trilby, only to find the enormous hat taking her own measurements. She recorded them in a tiny ledger, and the fact that the numbers were always the same did nothing to stop her: By her death, the book would have hundreds of columns, all of which testified that her waist size had never changed.

The two women were inseparable. They were almost twenty years apart, and neither had any family. Mon gros chapeau's parents had died long ago, and her in-laws lived several provinces away. Mon petit flétan, meanwhile, had a school of brothers, all in the navy, all somewhere at sea. They agreed to take turns keeping their husbands' letters, so that half stayed with one Marie and half with the other. This forced them to forget their earlier jealousy and adopt a certain level of trust. Though they vowed to never read anything they shouldn't, it was a promise each woman expected the other to break. Since both assumed their innermost secrets were already known, they could hardly help clinging together for the entire length of the war.

The first great secret imparted by mon petit flétan was that her loyalty to the fisherman was not as firm as she had led the men in town to believe. Aside from gutting fish, she had little to keep herself occupied. In times of war, she said, loneliness is the only thing that can thrive. She confessed that she suffered from erotic dreams, strange longings, and an indefinable attraction to the man who sold the ice. She lived in mortal terror of a heat wave, for she was certain the sight of the ice man in sweat would be enough to make her crack.

Although mon gros chapeau had nothing against adultery, she could not endorse an affair with the ice man. She had a general mistrust for any man under fifty who was not a soldier — she was certain they must be criminals, cowards, cripples, or some combination thereof. She cautioned the little halibut that the only acceptable lovers were pentagenarians or beyond. She further advised that any man who lived in town was also out of the question. It was clear she had been considering the question for some time. This was her great secret: Well aware that she could not keep her miscarriage a secret forever, she had decided to take a lover.

If I act quickly enough, she said, Jean will never know the truth. It's a well known fact that men are incapable of telling the true age of any child under three. Mon petit flétan replied that this was an old wives' tale, but the enormous hat was convinced it was true. My father, she declared, could never tell the difference between an infant and a toddler of two.

Together, the two women eyed the migrants, the wanderers, the travelling salesmen, but neither ever acted. Mon gros chapeau, unable to shake her suspicion of any man not at war, was never able to select an appropriate father. At last, she sent a letter to the milliner. It was no coincidence that the postmark was a year and a day since her miscarriage — the proper mourning period, she said, does not change no matter how long you knew the dead. In the letter, she told her husband that crib death had claimed their tiny son, and wrote with such clarity about the boy that she almost came to believe he had actually existed.

As for the little halibut, she tiptoed to adultery but never quite reached it. She never once truly considered the transients; for her, the ice man was the only one who held any appeal. On the days when he came, she made sure to wear a pretty dress. She wore rouge. She tossed her hair. But she never dared go any further, and after he was gone, she'd stare at the drops he had left behind and wonder miserably if they were water or his sweat.

In the second year of the war, the enormous hat began to lose her sight. The cataracts fell over her like drops of milk until her vision was completely obscured. She should have learned her lesson, but some people never do, and like the secret of her miscarriage, she kept it to herself until it was too late.

When she could no longer read her husband's letters, she went to Sylvie Manon, the prostitute known for both her literacy and her discretion. It was a terrible mistake. Sylvie Manon had been receiving love letters for years; she was one of those fantastic prostitutes who was so adept that men had to woo her just to get an appointment. An expert on epistolary romance, she took one look at the milliner's letter and declared that it could only have been written by a man not in love.

Mon gros chapeau did not want to believe her. She insisted the letter was an aberration, perhaps written during hunger or fatigue. But when the next two letters received a similar verdict, the enormous hat finally grew scared. Those long-held doubts of her husband's sincerity returned. The next time a letter came, she did not go to Sylvie Manon, but instead finally took mon petit flétan into her confidence. The secret did not surprise the little halibut. She already suspected something was amiss: The other Marie was a woman whose hats had always matched her outfits, and lately the colors had begun to clash.

Read this, begged mon gros chapeau. And tell me if you think it was written by a man in love.

Mon petit flétan read the letter. The other side, the one from her fisherman, spoke little of the war. It was a daydream composed entirely of what they would do when he returned. It ended with an anecdote: While marching, he had, by chance, smelled some halibut and thought of her. By contrast, the milliner's letter was so technical it might have been a military report. He wrote only of routine, the sun-to-moon tedium, and the constant yearning for a fresh pair of socks. The little halibut lowered the page. She did not need to be a prostitute to know a letter written from habit and not desire.

I think he loves you very much, she said, but she was a terrible liar, and mon gros chapeau was not convinced.

Before long, the blind woman refused to leave her house. Nothing is where it should be, she declared, as if the world was rearranging itself on whim. She closed the millinery, and within a year, the town's hats fell into disrepute. The tailors did what they could, but many headpieces were never the same. Veils hung by a thread, while old straw hats were fed to the cows. Feathers and bows fell loose and floated on the brims. During a wedding, nearly a dozen false roses fell to the ground when the guests simultaneously bent to reach for a tissue.

The enormous hat trusted no one but mon petit flétan to be her guide; having lost faith in her ability to distinguish one part of the world from another, she no longer believed she could even tell an apple from a pear. The little halibut did not mind the arrangement. The other Marie provided her with distraction and a feeling of worth. After work, she would stand in the *poissonnerie*'s water closet and scrub herself as vigorously as she had once done before a date with Jean. Mon gros chapeau's sense of smell had become miraculous overnight, and the little halibut emerged so coiffed and fragrant that men in town believed someone had finally snared her. Even the enormous hat did not realize what was being done for her benefit; one afternoon, she went so far as to accuse her friend of finally succumbing to the ice man's sweat.

Unable to read her husband's letters, mon gros chapeau found she still wanted to recall what they said. She decided on an astounding feat: She would commit three and a half years of letters completely to memory. There were almost a hundred of them by then, and each day mon petit flétan would come and read a few sentences, which mon gros chapeau would repeat back until she knew them by heart. The newer letters were the easiest to learn, for they had become as short as a haiku. But at least haikus are pretty; these were such terrible, unlovely things that she wondered if they had been written under duress. It was no wonder that she preferred the distant past to the recent one, which is to say the letters written when her husband still believed he had a son.

In her own letters, the little halibut pleaded with her husband to tell the milliner to write about something other than the weather. Her husband's reply was as sad as it was blunt: It's a miracle he's writing at all, he said.

One afternoon, the handwriting changed. Mon petit flétan had become something of an expert, and quickly saw that while the fisherman's vowels were the same, the milliner's O's were not quite as round as they once were. On the other side of the page, her husband explained why: A week earlier, the milliner had failed to appear after a battle, and many assumed he was either dead or captured. There was, however, also a persistent rumor that he had deserted after falling in love. The fisherman had written to mon gros chapeau himself, because until he knew the truth he did not want to cause unnecessary concern.

How would the concern be unnecessary? wondered mon petit flétan. Dead, captured or in love with someone else — all three seemed reason enough to worry. Still, she recognized in the gesture the very compassion that had made her love her husband, and she knew in that moment that she could stay loyal until the end of the war, no matter how much the ice man sweated.

The second time she read the letter, she realized that neither soldier knew mon gros chapeau had gone blind. The little halibut had never told her husband, and as usual, mon gros chapeau had been observing the proper mourning period before revealing the truth. Mon petit flétan dutifully read the false letter to her neighbor, and later wrote her husband to tell him that if he had to forge another letter, it would not be necessary to go through the trouble of imitating the milliner's O's.

The next time a letter came, it bore a shocking phrase: Á mon petit flétan. Mon gros chapeau was not mentioned at all. The gossipy postman went wild with the news. Fortunately, the enormous hat had become such a recluse that she never heard a thing. Mon petit flétan hurriedly dashed off a letter to the front, chastising her husband for his foolishness. For the next several weeks, the mistake was corrected. Although the letter had words meant only for the little halibut, the envelope was once again addressed to the two Maries. Mon petit flétan kept these letters to herself. When the enormous hat remarked that it had been a while since they had heard from the men, the little halibut merely shrugged.

Any day now, she said. War affects postmen too.

Then, just like that, the war ended. Even in isolation, mon gros chapeau heard the news. Peace is a noisy thing; there was revelry in the streets and the cries of women as the men began to return. Not all the cries were happy ones — many had come to see the absence of men as something of a blessing — but in all cases the cries were loud, so loud that the enormous hat could not help hearing them and realized her milliner was coming home.

She begged the little halibut to brush her hair. She asked all sorts of questions, terrified she had gone gray and ugly during her months in the dark. The only thing she was certain of was her waist; she had been measuring things for so long that she knew the size by the length of the tape.

He won't care how you look, said the little halibut. She was fumbling with the brush.

Of course he'll care, snapped mon gros chapeau. You think that they won't care, just because they haven't seen us? Imagine fighting all this time, only to come home and be disappointed.

Mon petit flétan should have taken that moment to tell the truth, but instead she went home to study her soft belly and hair of blackish-gray. She stood in the mirror and sniffed herself. As always, she had scrubbed for mon gros chapeau, but she thought a whisper of fish still lingered. She did not think her fisherman would be disappointed, but how can you predict disappointment? He had once been accustomed to halibut, but maybe he'd return and find the scent had become a stench.

Outside, she heard the familiar rattle of the ice man's truck. The ice man. She did not fix her hair or rouge her face. Instead, she went as she was, plain and unadorned, smelling vaguely of fish. If he still smiles at me, she thought, I'll know I'm no disappointment. He rapped lightly on the door, but when she opened it, she saw it was not the ice man at all, but her fisherman, trim and neat, a medal of heroism pinned to his breast. The ice man's truck sat in the driveway — he had given the fisherman a lift from the train station.

She did not speak or dare to move, not until her husband fell into her, breathed her scent and sighed.

Later, he told her the truth about the milliner. He had, as so many suspected, deserted after falling in love with a German farm girl. After that, said the fisherman, he was destined to be shot, if not by his own people, then certainly by the girl's husband. As was, he got lucky. Some of us found him after an air raid. I recognized him, but didn't say anything. A mass grave is better than a court martial. And they don't give pensions to the wives of traitors …

You lied to them, said the little halibut slowly.

Oh, I'm quite the liar now, said the fisherman. He fingered his medal of honor. You think I deserved this? What did I do except kill people? That's not a hero. War makes liars of us all.

Peace, too, said mon petit flétan, and in her head, she began to compose a letter.

That night, mon petit flétan practiced telling her husband all manners of untruths. She lay in bed and told the most colossal lies she could think of. When the fisherman was finally impressed, she went next door. In her hands was a letter from the milliner, one written entirely from scratch.

The new letter had none of the tedium of its predecessors. Mon gros chapeau listened as her husband explained that he would have to stay overseas a little longer. He apologized for being distant and cold and he proclaimed nothing but true love and declared a passion she had not seen since that first day he had measured her for a hat.

She was instantly suspicious. Read me what he really wrote, she said.

But this is what he wrote, insisted mon petit flétan. Rehearsal paid off: Her voice did not quiver at all.

The enormous hat was still unsure. She demanded to be taken to Sylvie Manon.

Mon petit flétan held her breath the entire way. Although she had actually written a letter, she had not bothered to disguise the handwriting, and the paper was clearly the sort found in the corner store. But Sylvie Manon did not notice either thing, or if she did, her notorious discretion kept her from admitting it. She read the letter out loud and smiled from one rouged cheek to the other:

Now here is a thing written by someone in love, she said. Technically, it was not a lie.

After that, mon gros chapeau believed every word the little halibut ever read. Her only other remark was that her husband must be learning something other than how to fight, for his vocabulary had greatly improved.

In a few short months, mon petit flétan went from a terrible liar to an expert one. The milliner's letters were the finest he ever wrote, which was only to be expected — they had been composed by not one lover, but two. With the fisherman's help, the little halibut was able to perfectly describe a battered Europe still in need of a gallant milliner. They invented all sorts of heroism. Like Hollywood, they championed bravado and ignored death. Mon petit flétan dealt with dead things all day, leaving her no patience for them in her prose. If her invented letters had been the only surviving record of the war, then it would have been remembered as the most amazing campaign ever, with the greatest heroics and the fewest funerals.

The effect of the lie could not be denied. Suddenly happier, mon gros chapeau returned to repairing the town's hats. She was pleased to find her skills were so honed she could work mostly by touch. She also continued to write to the milliner. She recited the letters to mon petit flétan, who wrote them down, but of course never put them in the mail.

They were kept in a drawer by the little halibut's bed, who would refer to them when composing the replies so she could address any remarks the other Marie had made. In not a single letter did the enormous hat ever admit she was having trouble with her sight. I'll tell him in my own time, she told mon petit flétan, but the truth was she was still hoping that her vision would miraculously return.

Eventually, the army declared the milliner officially dead. They sent along his pension, which the little halibut quietly cashed; no one thought this strange, since the banks were already used to her acting on the other Marie's behalf. Mon gros chapeau's reluctance to leave the house further helped the story along, but the true blessing was the departure of the gossipy postmaster, who was replaced by someone who mostly kept to himself.

Most lies end with the truth, but this one ended with a bout of pneumonia, which claimed the enormous hat the following Christmas. She was in the hospital when she learned she did not have long to live. Wanting to dictate a final letter to her husband, she called for the little halibut, who drove to her with the fisherman in their battered truck. It was here that mon petit flétan was seized with a tremendous need to reveal the truth. Never religious, she was nonetheless struck by the terrible vision of the enormous hat reaching the afterlife, only to find the milliner in the arms of a German farm girl. She entered the hospital determined to announce that a message had just arrived informing them of the milliner's death.

She's done for anyway, she told the fisherman. At least this way she'll be prepared. At least this way, if she sees him, she won't be surprised.

But when they reached the room, mon gros chapeau was already gone, and whether or not she was surprised in the afterlife, no one really knows.

The fisherman and his wife returned to town, where she remained his little halibut for many years. This was mostly out of practicality, for they had named their first girl after the milliner's wife, and both knew that a *nom de guerre* was the best way to avoid confusion.

ELIJAH

Lisa Locascio

Fiction

The summer after your first year of high school you are supposed to marry a boy with a fat pink mouth and an active tongue. You meet him one September night when he is playing guitar in a conference room at the public library. Janet Marshall, whose hair will later become one huge dreadlock, tells you, "Elijah has these parties, he calls them shows, but they're just parties, and he plays songs." He crouches over a guitar, humming and mumbling, occasionally emitting an intelligible word, "The end/a friend/you send/mend," as he hits the thickest string of his instrument. Janet whispers: "You know how he just said 'a friend?' I'm the friend." You are wearing the sexiest thing you own, a leopard print skirt edged in black lace. "Hey," he says to you after the song.

He invites you to Denny's after the show. When your dad comes to pick you up, you ask to go. Elijah stands behind you with his guitar tucked under his arm. "I'll walk home," you tell your dad, who says, "I don't think so, sweetie," lowering his eyes to show you that he's exhausted. The next week at school Elijah has Janet deliver a note to you. It is signed with a giant S that forms the first letter of his closing phrase, "Sorry So Short and Shitty." Then he calls you on the phone. His voice is like a caterpillar climbing into your ear. The bathroom floor blazes up under your feet when you look in the mirror, and you stamp and stamp. You dance.

He comes to your door on a Sunday afternoon to walk you to the movie theater where you have always been driven. You close your eyes to listen to his stories about the day he will get his driver's license. During the movie, he kisses you and kisses you. You think you will slide off the seat. You are not a person anymore, only a mouth. He takes you back to his house and kisses you more as you stand on the tile floor that he helped his father install. His parents grin at you on the drive home because they know who their son is, what he does.

Elijah shrink wraps fruit after school at Certified Land Grocery. His boss Vinnie loves him because Elijah brings Vinnie tuxedo condoms. In return, Vinnie slips Elijah an unmarked VHS compilation of pornography that you watch in your new boyfriend's basement. You hang out with his friends in his backyard on Tuesday afternoons; he sits at a picnic table under an umbrella and plays his electric guitar without an amp. He brags about the pickups on the guitar, and you smile at a guy named Big Black Mark like you know what that means. You take lessons at a school called Guitar Fun, you can play, too, but your boyfriend takes the instrument out of your hands. "Someday," he says, "I'll teach you how to really play."

He says his contacts are the reason for his constant blinking. He tells you that you gave him acne by holding your face so close to his. He brings over an old pair of cowboy boots, puts them on your feet, and introduces you to biting for pleasure. He runs up to you in the hall at school and asks for money to eat at a restaurant he calls Tasty Frog.

You go to the park where you played as a child and hang from the monkey bars with him. Down in your basement he snakes his hand across your body to cup your breast under your bra. He asks if it is okay, and it is. You ditch Janet and her date at homecoming and go to Denny's, instead, where you and another couple suck face for hours over a carafe of orange juice. He presses you against the jukebox in his basement again and put his hands on your hips, then takes you to the couch and reaches into your pants. "Is this okay?" You nod against your full mouth.

When he was eleven years old he lost his virginity to a girl in Denver who was a stranger to him. The next morning she put on the song 'Soothe' and shot herself when he was at the airport waiting for his flight back to O'Hare. This is why he can't listen to that song. The police came to get him at the gate and he had to identify the body. Another time, he made so much money selling drugs that he bought a ticket to Alaska just because it was far away. He called his dad from the Anchorage airport and asked, "Guess where I am?"

He is bisexual. He has been homeless. He has watched a boy drink a handful of liquid LSD and be taken screaming to the local psych ward. The world he tells you about, where girls cut their wrists in apartments he rented in the eighth grade, does not match the maid dusting fringed antique lamps in his living room or his waxed eyebrows, which he has done while his mom gets her perms. He waxes them, he says, because he doesn't do enough to make his mother happy. But you cry when he cries. You tell your friends, "I cannot believe what he has gone through."

One week you lose your virginity under a *Trainspotting* poster, the next he wants you to dress up for sex and pretend to be thirteen, one year younger than your real age, and by the following Tuesday he has raided his mother's dildo collection. You watch him shower, during which he washes his penis for twenty minutes and the rest of his body for thirty seconds. Between second and third period one day, he pulls what looks like ketchup packets from his pockets. They are filled with cinnamon scented lubricant. Your pants smell like Cinnabon for weeks afterwards. As you come out of his basement one night, his father chuckles and says, "You should see what your hair looks like." His mother nicknames you My Little Pony.

The sweetest thing he ever does for you is let you buy him a pleated black kilt. You have a thing about men in skirts. He can't keep the kilt at his house because of his dad, so he has you bring it in a Jewel bag to a poetry reading in Wicker Park. The neighborhood is still currency exchanges and liquor stores, no coffee shops or eyebrow threading salons yet, and your mom is not happy dropping you off, but she does. He changes into the kilt in the bathroom, sends you out into the night to find a payphone to call for a ride home, gropes you in the corridor. He becomes angry, then sad. "Sorry, baby," he says. "I haven't touched you enough today." Then he takes you in the bathroom and fingers you in a stall. Who is more surprised, you or Elijah, when you come violently on his hand?

He thinks he is teaching you things. At his direction you cut off your long hair and bleach it the color of the heat lightning on the rural highway that leads to your family's summer home. You talk about the hand-binding ceremony you will have that July — a pagan wedding, because you are both Wiccans. You buy a heavy black dress and tell your mother, "Well, today I chose the dress I will probably be married in." He gets his driver's license and comes over. Your father says, "You know, I would like it if he asked me to take you for a ride. And I would like it if just once, when he wants you to do something, you said no." He looks down, again. He's tired of you.

Your boyfriend declares that your father is his worst enemy. "After we're married, we might see your mom sometimes, but not your dad. Ever," he says. Then he asks your father if he can take you for a ride. Your father rolls his eyes but says yes, so Elijah drives you to Rolling Stone Records up on Irving Park Road, sticking his tongue out for you to lean over and kiss on the way.

Later that evening, in your living room, which is undergoing renovation, Elijah kisses you full on the mouth, takes your hand and presses it into his best friend's crotch. Your parents are out late at a movie. You and the best friend look at Elijah, who slits his eyes and says, "Let's have a threesome." You take off your clothes and kneel in front of Elijah, lick his fly. When he is in your mouth, his best friend is behind you, trying to enter. It does not work. You keep trying, smiling around Elijah and moving enthusiastically, but nothing fits. Your feet slip on the plastic tarp on the floor. You turn and look at the best friend, who shrugs and winks, and both of you put your clothes back on.

When you're alone, Elijah cries about how you want to have sex with his best friend. You tell him you don't, but you think about it and you do. You liked the way he gave up so quickly. It's like he gave you a rain check. And when you see him in the hall at school he crouches a little to say hello to you — he's very tall — instead of running up to you and mauling you with his tongue, like Elijah does.

Elijah has taught you things after all. His best friend starts coming over to your house in the middle of the night. You stage a scavenger hunt for places to have sex with his best friend in your house at two, three, four o'clock in the morning: a too-small couch in the junk room, a discarded chair, the downstairs hallway. On Easter Sunday you go to his best friend's house at the darkest part of the night and walk back at dawn, your hair matted and your eyes silver.

After a month of this, you break up with Elijah. He sits on your doorstep and cries and cries, but in your mind you replay the moment when you put a cough drop in your mouth and gave it that way to his best friend. His hair was soft in your hands, and he smelled strongly of something wonderful, of good weather, you thought as you sucked on his mouth.

He sends his little brother and a friend to collect the things he lent you, a journal full of drawings of girls pulling up their skirts, the tiny white teddy bear he has loved since infancy, a rare, band T-shirt that reads FUCK YOU AN ODE TO NO ONE. When the brother and the friend ask for it, they shout these words at you, as they have clearly been instructed to do. They also take the heavy choke chain that belonged to his deceased standard poodle and hung around your neck for seven months, a necklace anchored by an enormous metal clip. When you walked, the clip knocked into your breastplate, leaving a green shadow on your skin that grew darker and darker because you never took it off.

They leave with his things. You sit on your stairs and remember an October weekend at the beginning of all of this, when you went on a trip to Michigan with your family. When you came back you wanted to go see him. Your father resisted, and you shouted, "I have a boyfriend, okay? I don't want to hide it anymore!" But you had never hidden it at all.

You went to Elijah and pulled out the journal in which you had begun to write. It said SLUT on one side, VIRGIN on the other. You read a multi-part essay to him that you started in Michigan. It was about a wasp sting, football, a sweater the color of canned corn. And then: "How strange it is that only a month before I did not even know who Elijah was, that he was not even a flicker on the back of my eye. I remember when I was little and didn't know my best friend yet," you wrote. He stopped you there and touched your body. "I want to hear more about me," he said.

CUMBERLAND REUNION
Dave Smith

To her last prom, the final high school reunion, I drove
my mother, arthritic, widowed, wanting to see
as we climbed Cumberland's hills, gray
men shuffling to work, coming home as
afternoon sun pressed hard over those
so few they made one class. Then up the broken
streets, cars lodged hull to hull, wheels tucked in,
garbage in gutters bricked the old way. Few faces here

she sighed, Fridays here they start weekends early.
Row houses block after block, and bars freckling
the dark solitudes, in windows neon come-ons.
I could see perched on stools a clutch
of darlings, heads turning as slowly
we passed, each one she might have refused
a mirror's flicker, day waning, ball caps
soiled and low. Which one is he? I wanted to ask.

On we climbed until, puffing, she giggled and pointed
me inside. She wants to show me off, I thought,
sweating, and now, at jukebox, she twisted a little,
reciting phrases, lines gone to war, words not spoken
until, floor crying, scrape of raw shoes, <u>Drink, Lady?</u>
Then light we stood in so suddenly. One hawked,
stools spun, some old boys laughed back into tales

they couldn't escape. Smoke hummed from the hole
of each next bar, so we walked on. There were trees,
she said, the river smelled, my room was too close,
I saw ducks ride away, snow came. Your father
wanted to go, so we went. Street lights
flicked on. She seemed lighter now, heels
skipping, almost, over cobblestones. They'll see

your father in you, she'd said. Crossing B&O tracks
where they'd all been carried away, the dead
G.I.s, swells, ladies, the porters in black,
music I hadn't heard yet pushing them on,
I imagined, sweetly powdered, the white heads
bending into the hotel where they had been
once forbidden to go, shawled, slender girls

swaying as a tune needled them. In the deep blue above
mountains like walls stars loomed clear and boyish.
My heart ticked from going up Second Street.
Sweating, I thought how they'd be waiting,
the last ones, eyes made up, the first
glance of something they hadn't known,
big red hands reaching to them, like mine, fumbling.

LEARNING TO FLY IN MILLER'S FIELD
Steve Tompkins

Taken away by the feeling
of those silver-tasseled seed stems
sliding across my outstretched arms
and slipping through my fingers
like warm ribbons of rain,
I closed my eyes and began to fly
through Miller's field of Indian grass.

But the Mackey brothers,
breathing hard and rushing up behind,
brought me back down to earth
when they caught me
five strides from the fence
and a hundred yards from home
with a rock to the back of my head.

I could have fought back.
Perhaps I should have fought back.
Instead, when my father berated me
and demanded to know why
I let them beat me and did nothing
to stop it, I stood up and told him
that none of that really mattered.
I had risen up to face them
with my arms opened wide, I said,
because I knew how to fly.

FEAR OF LAUGHTER
Samira Grace Didos

After my mother and her two sisters were stripped
of the sure walls that held their lives,
and the gentlest of them received news
that the man she loved was killed
four months after they were married —
they learned to fear laughter.

It's like they were afraid
to let go of vigilance,
reluctant to let go of loss,
anxious that misfortune's fist
would swing and strike them again.

After catastrophe, joy hibernates
in heart's dark and boarded-up spaces
lest feelings of ease slink in
and gnaw the fragile shield
set against the unseen,
but surely coming storm.

BILLBOARD
Robert Nazarene

Nobody seen him coming or'd say if they did.
— Anonymous witness

I couldn't swear it was him on the shoulder of I-80
in a whiteout of snow, icicles
forming in his beard.

      If you own a photograph

of him braving this hell — or, perhaps, a holograph —
please show it to me.
I wonder if his flock would have followed him to take a meal
in a crummy roadside truck stop — in a bandaged-together,
leatherette booth? — a quarter-a-play jukebox
perched like Humpty-Dumpty on the window ledge.

      And what if somewhere

in the stack of folding cards there appeared Porter Waggoner's
#1 Billboard tune: *If Jesus Came to Spend Some Time with You*?
Or maybe Dolly Parton's chart-topper: *Coat of Many Colors*?
Would you have drawn his attention to the piss
thawing from his jeans and running down his legs?

      What comes next

is far easier to decide in a state of fear. The side of an Interstate
in an Iowa whiteout can be a loveless place, Thank You Jesus
— no matter which side of the window you're on.
And therein lies the question.

      Close by, a flock of sheep

is meekly dying, preparing to inherit the Earth
in a field beneath an enormous
white and green billboard proclaiming
His Name — close enough
to kiss.

INHERITANCE
Donna Pucciani

These tendrils disdain the sheen of fashion,
curl like spooning lovers, speak the language
of silkworms, not lank strands runway sleek.
These tresses love wind, not comb,
quiver like chinchillas, like the tails of piglets
or the trails of comets, the inherited filigree
of a grandmother's necklace, beard of an uncle
I never knew.

Spanish moss festoons live oak trees in hot winds
off the Gulf, where mother stayed out all night
and sang at the harbor fishermen's Mass
wearing Sunday dawn in her blue satin gown,
where the tangled hair of mermaids borrowed
whorls from conch, seaweed from barnacles.

Like the coast road above Amalfi Bay,
a corkscrew in a peasant bardolino,
or papa's gemelli that holds sauce well,
the hair of a New York Italian princess
curls soft as fine wool on a crochet hook,
thick as moss impervious to fingers,
cornsilk awry, alfalfa sprouts,
or bits of ribbon tucked in a bird's nest.

I wind it around my index finger, remembering
a mad alcoholic voodoo mother and a brilliant
gentle father with black ringlets middle-parted
under an army hat or crowding his big-hearted chest.

Squiggling sperm gave its own shape
to this headful of fluff and frivolity that is
not me, that in the rain, sticks to my wondering cheek
the way smoke wraps air, past invades future.
To own it is not a choice. One must lose control,
relinquish oneself to coiled DNA sprung
from the Hudson River, Lake Pontchartrain,
and the hot Calabrian sea.

THE CIRCLE REINVENTING ITSELF
Jackie Bartley

Touch me. Remind me who I am. — Stanley Kunitz

Clutches of large flowered bellwort bloom in spring,
bending as if beneath a current's flow,
making *slouch* look lovely, not the stand-up-straight
my mother preached. They droop with a wantonness
I wish I possessed.
                              My mother as a girl: her father taken
by syphilis, cast out. The terrible order of that house
once he was gone: *We must not embrace*, her mother said.
How could my grandmother have gotten it so wrong?

From that day on, she would not hug her children,
forbade them from touching her, from touching one another.
Three of them growing like rocks in a dry streambed.
Their childhood scoured smooth, no place to hold.
Then, the war, and for each of them, marriage, a child.

Cousins not knowing till we'd grown
why relationships plunged us, limp with desire,
into white water hydraulics
or stiffened and broke us as if we were standing waves.
Wanting to be embraced, to float, womblike,
in the presence of another.

For years, I grew heavy in the brilliance of green spring
and believed what I most wanted
could never be. Though, now, it comes mostly in dreams,
and I wake stained with memories I do not believe
are my own. And, still, I do not know how to *make* love
fluid like a stream yet solid as stone. I only remember
she held me once in water, and her arms
buoyed me along as she taught me to swim.
Like Miriam, she abandoned me
to the current. And I left her arms and I swam
and did not drown.

PAINTING WITH THE DEAD
Mark Liebenow

Johannes Vermeer, The Milkmaid, 1658

Grind the dead bodies
of female cochineal insects.
Boil. Extract the red.

Distill the mucus of snails
for the purple preferred
by Roman emperors.

Pulverize semi-precious stones,
lapis lazuli for the radiant blue Vermeer used
in the resigned milkmaid's apron.

Indian yellow for her blouse
from the urine of cattle
fed only mango leaves.

Egyptian brown squeezed
from the wrappings of mummies,
until these ancients oozed dry.

Bind the colors to canvas
with drippings of animal fat,
egg white, curdled milk or wax.

I lower the shades,
sift cremated flakes scraped
from the painting of our marriage,

rearrange the scraps
of what death has left
for the living of one.

Stretching the shroud of new canvas,
I collect burnt skin,
grind iron oxides with ossified bone,

stir falling light into death's decay,
paint darkness as it hardens
and sets.

THE AMAZING MR. MUSCLE   *Fiction*
Ryan Mecklenburg

The doctor explained that lung cancer was a malignant growth and no, it wasn't something Mr. Vignor had contracted sexually. Years of smoking was likely the cause so Mr. Vignor, or as the doctor preferred to put it, *we* should be careful with how *we* treated *our* lungs. Using a pull-down map on the office wall, which read: THE RESPIRATORY SYSTEM, the doctor pointed a pen at the leafless tree growing upside down from the drawing's throat and explained how the cancer grew across the countless ramifications like small buds when *we* wanted bare winter branches.

Mr. Vignor's niece, Darla, was there and held his hand. She was a mother and wife in her mid-thirties, but he always saw that childish face beneath the wrinkles that were creeping in. Her green eyes seemed so much larger, he thought, because of her slim frame. Even after two children, she had a nice figure and a smile that lit up her face whenever they met.

Then treatments were named: Chemotherapy using antimetabolites, cryosurgery, radiation, surgery removing portions of the lung, perhaps even monochlonal antibodies; a list that mystified him. But it was expected this late in life; it came with his short hair graying and the blueness of his eyes dulling. He looked older than he was, something this doctor would blame on smoking because he blamed everything else on Mr. Vignor's one pleasure.

To further demonstrate the deterioration of his lungs, the doctor had him blow into a hose connected to a tube with a red ball. Healthy men, according to the doctor, got the ball to the tube's fourth or fifth hatch mark. Mr. Vignor couldn't pass the first, which sold Darla on the diagnosis. With the encouragement of his doctor and niece, and despite his own disdain for this rigmarole, Mr. Vignor, or rather, his insurance company, opted for the radiation and chemotherapy.

In the show's heyday, Buddy, the manager, an ugly man with pockmarks and a bulbous nose, called him Viggie and often met with him in the office to discuss the act and disseminate advice. On one occasion, Buddy sat back in the chair at his desk and explained that Viggie needed to better consider who he let into his trailer. No telling what disease one of these women, who visited as the circus traveled from town to town, might carry. Sure, Buddy had had his fill of women back in the day, he gladly admitted, but caution still needed its payment. Viggie understood, but when he came upon one of them at his trailer door, one thing led to the next.

Buddy didn't preach long before he rolled the newest poster across his desk. Arched across the top, in red letters: THE AMAZING MR. MUSCLE. Underneath was Viggie's caricature, small feet and legs blooming into a bushy physique of toned muscles and flexed arms. As usual, the bald head was shinier than Viggie could ever polish it, and his curled mustache came out past his face. At the bottom were listed the feats performed on stage: The Telephone Book Tear, The Imploding Beer Can, The Leisurely Woman Lift (No weight of woman too great!), The dumbbells of 1,000 lbs!, The Exalted Elephant, and The Great Phantom-X Routine (Women and children Beware!). *We'll be on every phone pole*, Buddy said. *Maybe some shop windows. I'm talking with a guy about a billboard. We'll be everywhere.* Buddy was nowhere on the poster.

To drum up further publicity, Buddy set up a contest outside of the sideshow. It was a tall post with a steel ball and a bell on top. Viggie swung a sledgehammer down on the platform, and it shot the bearing up to ring the bell. Any man who could match his strength could get in for free. Men approached, rolling up their shirt sleeves, but few ever made it past the halfway marker on the pole. It sold tickets.

Two clowns, then a juggler, warmed up the audience. Using the flowers on their lapels, the clowns squirted members of the crowd; they hit each other with pies before hosing themselves down with pressurized soda water. The juggler handled an array of things, beginning with oranges and ending with axes he sharpened on stage as the grinding wheel shot sparks toward the crowd. And for the finale, he juggled fire then guzzled from a pint of alcohol and blew a ball of fire at the audience.

Meanwhile, Viggie prepared backstage. He did pushups and ran in place to swell his muscles. After the workout, he rubbed baby oil over his body and dabbed his head. The crowd roared and applauded the clowns then the juggler. Viggie knew he could do this all of his life. As long as there were people who came and cheered him, he would play Mr. Muscle. This was the reason he had left home at seventeen to join the circus. He began scooping animal shit then assisted in the concessions while he bulked up enough to present Buddy with the idea of a muscle man show. Now he was what? Thirty, thirty-one. And he couldn't think of anything better to do.

Viggie checked his props. He added a little white paint to the 1,000 on each dumbbell. They didn't weigh quite that much which Buddy said was okay as long as people believed they were that heavy. He checked the straps on the harness for the Leisurely Woman Lift then put a soft pack of cigarettes down the front of his leotard. His assistant in the show, Evelyn, was an elephant now chained to a stake in the ground. He went over to her, and she wrapped her trunk around his arm, wiping off the baby oil. He rubbed her behind the ear and stared into her eye. When she blinked, he watched the blackness shrink within the iris. The final applause rose from the crowd. Evelyn seemed to know that distinct praise and nodded her head. He knew it too. It was time to go on.

It was a couple of days before the first radiation session when the doctor gave Mr. Vignor an examination. He warned that once the chemo began, there would be little *we* could stomach and that *we* should stick to fruit and maybe Jell-O. Then he wiped his thumb at the yellow ends of Mr. Vignor's grey mustache, then wiped at the yellowed fingernail where Mr. Vignor favored holding a cigarette and suggested it would be a good idea if *we* quit smoking also.

Darla was waiting outside the examination room when he and the doctor stepped out. The doctor restated everything he had just said like his patient couldn't tell her himself. To each statement, Darla nodded her head and agreed that, yes, most definitely, her uncle needed to kick his habit. The doctor walked them to the elevator and shook their hands like this was a farewell before a launch into space. Every time this doctor opened his mouth, Darla took it so seriously. In the elevator, Mr. Vignor said he ought to stomp out of this hospital and never come back, but then Darla put her arm through his and that was all it took to calm him.

They stepped from the elevator like that, with her arm through his. That people might think she was the lover of this old man, who had probably won her over with small gifts and mature affection, he kind of liked. But he wasn't that old. He'd be fifty-five next year, when he could begin thinking about retirement from his job as head maintenance at the office building.

In the cafeteria, Darla urged him to eat all he wanted on account of what the doctor said, her treat. He found them a table outside on the patio. The sun was out, and there were a few thin clouds like steam from a tea pot ready to boil over. Darla brought him a couple plates of food on a tray; one with Salisbury steak and potatoes with mixed vegetables, and the other with a cheeseburger and French fries on the side. He looked at them and couldn't believe these hospitals. The doctors sat up in their examination rooms nodding their fingers at people about eating right and watching this and that in their diet but then they served this food that was absolutely off the diet list any doctor recommended.

Darla talked with him about being nervous, which, he assured her, he wasn't. He ate the steak then the hamburger before Darla could finish her own plate. It had been a long time since he ate like this, probably not since his days in the show all those years ago. Then Darla brought up moving him out of the small apartment where he lived and into her own house.

"I'm fine where I'm at," he said. "You and your husband have enough with the kids."

"We could add on," she said. "I'm going to need your help after you recuperate."

"You're good to me. I don't know why, but you are. And you don't have to make me feel useful when all of this is over."

"You've always been good to me, and I love you very much. I'm not trying to make you feel useful, I'm thinking of getting a job."

"What do you need a job for?"

Darla looked at his empty plates. "Do you want some pie?" she asked.

He nodded that that would be okay. "How about some of that peach? I love peach."

She went inside, and he watched her through the glass as she got back in line. He pulled a soft pack of cigarettes from his sock. There were a couple left, and the one he pulled out was wrinkled and split toward the end so that a bush of tobacco was protruding. The first puff of smoke went up into the air and caught on some breeze he couldn't feel. Nothing like the first drag after a big meal to relax him. With the filter pinched between his thumb and finger, he rolled it back and forth. It was a miracle drug, this small stick, something doctors should prescribe for stress relief instead of condemning it. There was little difference between the harm caused from this cigarette and what all of this radiation chemotherapy would do. Both were small dosages of harm to his body, so why not choose the one that gave him a little ease?

"What are you doing?" It was Darla, standing at the table with two small plates of pie.

He waved the smoke away as if that might be what was bothering her. "What?"

"I just went over how much I'm going to need you, and you sit there smoking."

He raised his hand to swear. "Honest, this will be my last one. Once these treatments begin, I'm finished."

"It's killing you," she said.

"It's not killing me." As if on cue, like his body was in rebellion against him and in alliance with Darla and that doctor, he began a deadly fit of whoops and coughs.

The applause ushered off the juggler. Then there was Buddy's voice, muffled back stage, announcing the feats Mr. Muscle would perform. The applause rose again with a drum roll, and Viggie took his place behind the curtain that would open on him flexing his arms, one up one down, like a sideways S.

He astonished the crowds, tearing phone books in half and crumpling full beer cans into accordions, the alcohol wetting his boots. The front of his black wrestler's outfit was cut low and exposed his hairy chest and nipples which stared from the foliage like eyes. The matching boots shined from the spit and polish rubbed into them. His contracted muscles were like bags of sand, hard and bulging. Even his mustache, thick and curled at the ends, looked like two arms flexed. Every evening, they came with ice cream and hot dogs, these crowds, to watch him on stage. He awed them with strength they had not seen in another human, and it made him happy.

The Leisurely Woman Lift was a contraption that fit over Mr. Muscle's head and rested on his shoulders. Off each shoulder was a wooden beam suspended with a swing. Women from the audience came on stage to sit three to a seat. To demonstrate the ease of lifting such weight, he pulled a cigarette from his leotard and smoked it, puffing rings and plumes from his nostrils. With the women suspended to either side of him, and the smoke wafting up and away, the crowds whooped and applauded.

The Exalted Elephant poster that decorated the side of the stage advertised him with arms locked like goal posts, holding an elephant overhead. Even if that wasn't how the trick went, Buddy assured Viggie that it was okay because it brought in the crowds.

Buddy led Evelyn, the ever yielding elephant with tiara rested on her brow, by a chain onto the stage beside Mr. Muscle. Through a megaphone, Buddy announced her astounding weight of 10,000 pounds, and if all went well, The Amazing Mr. Muscle would lift 5,000 of them, the equivalent of two cars. Head shining under the lights, Mr. Muscle stepped behind her. He took a deep breath then stooped down to wedge his hands under her back foot. From then on, Evelyn did most of the work. With his face red and body trembling, he appeared to lift her back end up into the air. It wasn't so; Evelyn had been trained to lift herself into a handstand. He pressed his hands to her belly. She looked from the crowd to Mr. Muscle to the crowd again, something else trainers had taught her and audiences interpreted as astonishment. The people went wild.

At the end of the night, sweaty, he brought a bag of hamburgers, a giant cola and bundle of bananas out to her cage. She leaned into his caresses behind her ears. On an upturned bucket, he sat to eat. Evelyn, a faithful girl, never let him down during a show. He felt bad the way Buddy paraded her out and announced her heft. But she wore that tiara beautifully and had nothing to be ashamed of. The hamburgers and bananas he tossed her she mixed with hay and swallowed whole. His own he washed down with gulps of cola.

Using the pull-down map of the respiratory system, the doctor outlined the procedures of radiation and chemotherapy in medical terms. They sounded exact and sophisticated, but summarized into simple words, the radiation blasted the lungs like a nuclear bomb and chemotherapy filled the body with toxins that killed what might have survived the nuclear fallout. Darla patted his hand, and the doctor assured him these treatments would do the trick.

The nurses allowed him underwear beneath his gown. Darla walked him to an office room. Inside, Darla stood with the radiologist behind a barrier of glass. It made him feel like an exhibit at the zoo. The radiologist directed him to the machine from a speaker in the ceiling. The number of warning labels on the side was astounding. The wattage alone, if this went wrong, would be the equivalent of a toaster in the bath. The ceiling lights shining off his head, he stepped toward the machine. Darla encouraged him with waves and hand gestures shaped into the universal OK. Waiting for the radiation to burn his insides red, he wanted to tremble and hide somewhere. The radiologist came on the speaker. *Mr. Vignor, please lift your arm and turn toward the machine. Now this won't hurt.* The machine clicked and he braced himself. When it stopped, he looked from the technician to Darla to the technician, unsure what happened, if anything. He was asked to turn a few more times, then Mr. Vignor was free to go.

A few days after the final radiation treatment, he sat on a gurney in a long room watching the IV bag drip poison into his bloodstream. It hung from a steel bar bent like a gallows he could push around the floor on tiny wheels. Darla sat next to him on another gurney and appeared distant as she stared at the point in his arm where the needle pierced the skin.

"Is this about the cigarettes?" he asked. "Because I'm gonna quit, really."

"I know," she said. But she said it so gravely yet so easily that he didn't believe her.

Then a sudden heaviness, like the pulls of sleep, came across his body. It was this stuff they pumped into him. Suddenly he felt apathetic to Darla as she began talking about her two children and how busy their lives were. He felt a question forming to ask about them but then it was covered by a blanket of coldness and unconcern. Then an idea formed somewhere about Darla's husband, something he had been suspecting, something he couldn't name, it was something about her not mentioning him in a long time. She was going on but he was too tired to understand, listen, or hear. The most he could concentrate on was his yellowed fingernail the doctor had tried to wipe clean. The yellowness had grown out some since he promised Darla he'd quit smoking. He longed for a cigarette to take the edge off this IV.

Then the nurse brought in his lunch and set it before him. It was a roast beef sandwich with some coleslaw. Darla tore it in half for him. But his mouth was just as apathetic to food. A chemical taste came as he salivated. When he brought the bit of sandwich into his mouth, he felt nauseous. Every bite tasted tainted so that he had to swallow despite the gagging. What he swallowed, forcefully, freely came up and down the front of him.

Sometimes the shows were a mix of emotions for him. He always drew a swell of pride in his chest at entertaining the crowds. But it would always be a little girl up on her father's shoulder or holding a balloon that reminded him of his brother and little Darla, whom he had never met. He hadn't seen his brother in over ten years. The last time, his brother was about to get married so Viggie had stopped by the apartment to meet his future sister-in-law, and even then Viggie had a suitcase and bus ticket in hand about to answer an advertisement about a job with some circus. And that was ten years ago. So it was after a show when he felt especially grief stricken or simply missed his brother that he called to catch up. It was always difficult talking with his sister-in-law, having met her once. Then his brother would get on the line, and they would talk for a good time. Then there was their little girl, his niece, Darla. She was this petite voice that breathed heavily into the receiver and giggled a lot. Before hanging up once, his sister-in-law mentioned that Darla had had to make a list of her heroes for school. She had listed Mary Tyler Moore, her Mommy, and Uncle Muscle.

That got him teary eyed once, lying alone in his trailer. This kid he had never met thought *him* some sort of person to look up to. After that he began sending her letters. He could never write more than a page, and the kid probably got bored with that. Instead of signing his name, he made two capital M's each sharing the same inner leg. In some of the towns where the show stopped, he would browse the drugstores for postcards. He had never had a child and had to guess what girls liked. It was usually flowers or kittens he scribbled on the back of and sent her. Once he found one of Mary Tyler Moore. He was most proud of that one.

With the radiation and chemotherapy, his hair fell out. The crowds: Some friends from work and his family, mostly Darla, visited his hospital bedside. The chemo made him weak so that the paperbacks they brought him he could barely keep open before the bindings pulled themselves shut. His lungs also were weak. When breathing became especially difficult, the staff brought in an apparatus with an accordion inside a glass cylinder that pumped his lungs. Numb to his bladder, he wet the bed. The nurses changed his sheets and gown which covered his front side, but left the back and fleshy buttocks exposed. The skin of his arms hung droopy. In the mornings, they came with a razor and cream, these nurses, to shave him. That they humored him like this, not putting a blade in the razor, made him sad.

Following his session of chemo, the nurse gave him a sponge bath, then wheeled him back to his room where Darla was waiting. Besides weakening him, the chemicals made him shiver and sweat all at once. His gown did little to keep him warm, so he pulled the thin hospital sheets and blanket over himself, covering all but his head. Darla pulled the curtain between them and the other patient. It shrunk the room into a small box Darla never seemed to notice but that made him feel cramped.

"Where are the kids today?" he asked. She used to bring her boy and girl, but they tired easily and crawled under the curtain to look up at the other patient.

"With their father," she said, then reached for a paperback on the bedside table. "How about I read to you?"

She held the book up to read. The chemicals working through his blood hadn't taken effect so he felt interested in what Darla was about to read. Then he noticed her hand. The ring finger was bare and had a lighter band of skin. He began to put it together in his head.

"You look upset," he said.

"I'm just tired trying to get used to this new job."

"I'm happy when you come out. But is it taking a toll on your family?"

"This is important. I need to be here." She looked through the pages like she was trying to find where she last read, then wouldn't stop flipping back and forth. It took some effort but he took his hand from under the covers and placed it on hers so that she stopped.

"You used to come and talk to me when you were little, remember. I don't think you said two words to your mother before you came out to tell me about your day. How was your day?"

She clamped her hands around the book. "We're getting divorced. I was waiting for all of this to be over before I told you."

"I'm sorry. Is it repairable?"

"I don't know. He says he wants a different life and wants the kids." She told him about her new apartment and job at the bank. They were officially separated, and she was scared to go over there because she thought he might have a girlfriend and she couldn't handle that.

It took so much for him to concentrate on every word Darla said now.

This used to be the highlight of his days so long ago and now he was too weak to listen. He caught a *children* here and a few discouraging words like *end of my life* and *I can't believe it*. But the details of it all he just couldn't catch. They flittered right there in front of him like butterflies, but he had no strength to put out his hands and bring them to him for closer examination. He didn't care but wanted to know precisely what she was saying all at the same time.

After eating with Evelyn, he bathed in the portable showers then walked back to his trailer. There was a woman with wavy brown hair, somewhere in her late thirties, at his steps, biting her fingernail. He only had a towel around his waist with a pair of flip-flops, and his chest hair was dripping. She stood there as if she had the most innocent intentions. What did he know, maybe she did. It wasn't clear why these women came, if it was the show or his physique. His best guess: They were lonely like him, and people in similar situations attracted each other. She bowed her head when she said hello. He held the door for her, and she came right in. The trailer was silver and shaped like a bullet with little room for more than a bed and table where the woman sat. She looked around without any apparent objection to the mess and told him about her two sons watching the trapeze and her husband who was working late. He sat on the bed, still in his towel, and told her about Darla's list of heroes. When the conversation lagged he flexed his bicep and asked if she'd like to squeeze it. Her touch was timid, barely a caress. He encouraged a good squeeze until she left white handprints and her nails scratched his skin. The invitation progressed to palming his shoulders and pecks, then dangerously high on his quads, her fingertips under the towel. Having touched every exposed muscle, she suddenly tucked her hands into her lap. He asked if she wanted to see him flex the one muscle nobody ever saw. When she asked, *Which is that?*, he dropped his towel.

Going on with girls like that finally came back on him. In the middle of the night, Buddy banged at Viggie's trailer door. In bed alone, he answered wrapped in a blanket. Buddy was flustered. Someone in the show had taken the sheriff's daughter, a girl not quite eighteen, to bed and now the law was coming. The circus tent had been collapsed and everyone ran around like there was a fire. Viggie took the stands out from under his trailer and hitched up the truck. With his things ready, he went to help break down the stage and load it. The animal handlers called him over to help with Evelyn. She was reeling back against the chain around her neck. He had them slacken the restraint while he approached and caressed her behind the ear. He patted her on the trunk and talked to her in a soft voice. It wasn't long before she had her trunk over his shoulder following him up the ramp and into the cage.

The caravan pulled onto the highway toward the state line. Zooming down the road, Viggie cracked the window to keep himself awake. He tried thinking back to the conversation with the sheriff's daughter. When he had asked she had said old enough, and he couldn't help but think so when she undid the towel for him. He slammed his fist against the steering wheel. He should've listened to Buddy about who he let into the trailer. You could catch some disease as easily as you could catch the police on your tail. As the caravan raced into the next state he could see the flashing lights in the side mirror and hear the faint sound of sirens.

Lying in his hospital bed with his eyes closed, he listened as Darla read from the paperback. The mob had begun threatening the ambitious young lawyer finally making a name for himself, wanting retribution for getting him into the firm. Darla read in a motherly way, firm but warm, and entranced him. The words lost any meaning and there was only the sound of her voice. He wrapped himself in it and nestled himself into that deep blackness that skirts sleep with her voice in the distance, lulling him.

Then the pain. He struck at his chest, and Darla screamed. The nurses came in and pulled Darla away from the bed. His lungs had collapsed, and the staff rushed him out toward the OR. They prepped him on the way, and Darla ran alongside holding his hand. The staff had a time pulling her away at the swinging doors. While the chaos went on above him, he tried to recall what his niece had read. But he couldn't. A syringe pricked him. An oxygen mask came over his face. The gown was ripped from his body, and he lay naked. None of it compared to the care Darla gave him. She could tranquilize with her voice. The way she would straighten his overturned gown collar; all of that should have been enough to heal him and bring him home.

Then the lights overhead flashed once more, and he could hear his niece outside the doors, sobbing.

The doctor made sure Mr. Vignor knew what luck it was to survive such trauma to the lungs. Mr. Vignor was able to breathe on his own now and was sitting in the doctor's office. The respiratory poster wasn't used to explain why further smoking was counterproductive to the chemotherapy. The doctor pulled up a chair next to his patient who couldn't stand this man so close. Staff had seen Mr. Vignor out in the patio smoking. It had to stop, especially after this scare with his chest. If he went on smoking, there would be nothing left of his lungs. But he felt apathetic to the doctor's pleas. Apparently if he went on like this, the only choice would be to cut out portions of the lung. Then Mr. Vignor would have to push around a machine for the rest of his life just to breathe. Either he got rid of the cigarettes, or the cigarettes got rid of him. He almost laughed at that. And this browbeating only made him want a smoke that much more. It would be so satisfying to allow the ash to hang as long as possible then blow the smoke in the doctor's face. Then the doctor asked for the cigarettes Mr. Vignor kept under his gown. This startled him, but he pulled them from the waistband of his boxers anyway. The doctor threw them in the metallic trashcan, causing it to ring, before he left to make his rounds. The cigarettes had landed straight up with the lid open so that he could see the white circular end of each filter. Then the doctor came back in just as Mr. Vignor reached into the waste basket.

He had smoked on stage as part of the act, then continuously once the show stopped attracting crowds. A simple sideshow of a man in a leotard no longer sold tickets now that television was on the rise. On top of that, Buddy had stopped printing the Amazing Mr. Muscle posters. He was leery of advertising Viggie anywhere since outrunning the state troopers and relocating the show to the other side of the Midwest. It depressed Viggie and made him feel apathetic to the world outside his trailer. The crowds shrunk and got more worked up over the juggling fire eater than Mr. Muscle. It made him sad to look on such dismal crowds. His performance on the stage was meager at best and Buddy told him so. He stopped exercising and working out. He ate more hamburgers than bananas and went to his trailer to eat instead of sharing with Evelyn. He even stopped practicing their routine together which led to his fumbling on stage. It depressed him to be in the show. Men began beating him when he swung that hammer. Sometimes he didn't even ring the bell. His body went from shapely to fat. And of course the women stopped showing up at his door.

Buddy accused him of drinking, but that wasn't the case. Viggie simply didn't see the point anymore and couldn't find the will to put as much into the show. Now he smoked through the entire routine. A few times during the Leisurely Woman Lift he toppled over with the women in the swings screaming.

Performing with Evelyn, he walked off stage and left her in a handstand. He felt guilty abandoning her like that, as if she deserved it. But he couldn't do it any longer. He wanted to. He wanted the crowds out there again and the cheering and that gasp the people made when he tore phone books and crushed beer cans.

Buddy took Viggie off the bill, and the sideshow dwindled to the clowns with pies once the fire eater found a bigger show to sign with. Buddy gave Viggie a job sweeping and helping to set up booths and the tents. His hair grew out now, but he didn't comb it and could only wear his pants comfortably if he left the waist button undone. He would clean the other animal cages, but not Evelyn's. He would have cleaned hers best but he didn't have the heart to have her trunk caress his shoulder again. It wasn't that he held anything against her, it was that he felt so horrible for abandoning someone so faithful to him.

Buddy called him into the office and showed him the books for the circus. The sideshow had been axed and now Buddy needed to cut some of the extra workers who weren't absolutely necessary. Viggie understood. Buddy gave him what he could from the safe to get him on his way. When the show got back on its feet, Viggie, old Viggie, was welcome back and maybe they could have Mr. Muscle come back or invent some new show. He took the money and asked for the promotional posters collecting dust in Buddy's office. He packed his trailer like the close of any other show and drove east, aimlessly.

The doctors finally cut his lungs to small slivers so he could only breathe by using a machine and placed him on the intensive care floor. He craved a cigarette and became impatient with the staff for keeping him in the hospital. He toppled his food when they set it before him and refused to eat so that he became thinner. He lost patience with the nurses, unable to humor them or have them humor him; he asked they not pretend to shave him. He remained kind as ever to his niece. She came frequently and sat for long hours after dropping the children off with their father. She sat at his bedside and watched his chest rise and fall to the sound of the machine. He was calm with her around, so the nurses allowed her to stay past visiting hours. She cleaned out his bedpan and helped the cleaning staff dust the room. Sometimes she read until he slept. When he was conscious, she fed him Jell-O and told him about her new apartment. She had decorated her son's room with those old Mr. Muscle posters of his.

Once ties with the show were severed, he was invited to park the trailer in his brother's backyard and stay as long as he needed. Of all the people he would see, he was most embarrassed to meet Darla and for her to find this fat mess of a man. But, Darla, ten at the time, hugged his thick waist and couldn't stop smiling.

His brother found him a job as a night janitor cleaning toilets and dusting furniture in office buildings. He slept most of the day and woke to Darla's soft knock at his trailer door in the afternoon when she presented him part of her after school snack. He brought out a chrome chair for her and he sat on the steps with his knees pulled to his belly. She told him about her day at school and recited random facts she had learned, kicking her feet under the seat. After a brownie or plate of orange wedges he smoked and talked about traveling with the sideshow and the many towns and cities he visited.

She made him flex his arms out so she could hang from them. When a new phone book arrived she rushed him the old one and squealed with delight as he tore it in half. The old advertisement posters he rolled out on his bed for her; she studied them for hours, asking about Evelyn and each feat listed. She came out to his trailer at nights just as he was going to work. She would cry about her parents fighting and beg to take her with him. There, she helped him dust and poured bleach into the toilets.

In later years, his brother kept the house, and Darla grew distant from her divorced parents, but always she kept a fascination for her uncle and talked with him late into the night about how she was determined to be unlike her parents and never divorce if she ever married. He listened to her and tried to be impartial. Ever trying to be responsible, he encouraged her to go to college even though he had dropped out of high school himself and refused to give her a cigarette the numerous times she asked for a puff. As a gift, when she went away to college, he gave her one of the old posters for her dorm room. It was the last Buddy had printed of him holding Evelyn up with one arm. When she came back for vacations she told him about her friends loving the old advertisement and some even offering money for it.

During those years, elementary through college, Darla brought friends back to the trailer. Always, she introduced him as her uncle, Mr. Muscle; and the way she said it implied the amazing.

THE SWEEPER

Terry Sanville

Fiction

From her cushioned perch high up inside the glass booth of a 1995 Johnston, Lucy can just make out the brushes spinning below her. But she hardly watches anymore, now content to rest strong, russet-brown forearms across the big, flat wheel and bump along pre-dawn boulevards as the stoplights flash amber.

"*Stupido pendejos*," she thinks and steers around two illegally parked cars — one a good-looking Honda, something like Ramon's, and the other a junker pickup on flat tires. When she first started sweeping three years before, Lucy would have told her supervisor to inform the cops about repeat offenders who ignored the "No Parking" signs that march along these traffic arteries. Eugene had warned her to back off.

"The streets are clean enough, Lucy — and besides, nobody's complaining."

But she still longs for straight wide streets with clear curb extending forever. With a gloved hand, Lucy reflexively eases back on the brush elevation lever; the road is high-crowned here, and the left side will bottom out unless properly adjusted. Personal paraphernalia fastened to the instrument panel bounces and sways as the Johnston burrows through the darkness: a broken rosary hooked over the kill switch, faded Polaroids, and an I.D. tag picturing a stocky brown woman wearing an orange jumpsuit with a long, chocolate braid. Lucy steals a quick glance at the bleached faces cracked with grins, two tiny ones and an old woman kneeling on a cobblestone veranda. The hint of a smile tugs at her full lips as she remembers being waist-high, proudly sweeping that porch with bound-together stalks of her father's finest broomcorn.

She motors through an intersection and narrowly avoids colliding with a drunk driver who must have thought the flashing red lights were meant for somebody else. She remembers to lean hard on the horn and is rewarded with a single-digit salute from the boozer as he speeds away.

After making a quick pass through the business district, she turns down a dark side street lined with sycamores that fill the gutters with their dinner-plate-sized leaves. Driving slowly now and hugging the curb, she crawls past a one-story stucco apartment with its front room glowing behind hospital-white curtains. Her right foot slips off the gas pedal, and she lets the machine crunch to a stop. The Johnston's halogen beams illuminate a black sheen that spreads out across the sidewalk and flows into the street. Lucy traces the path of the flow as it streams from under a battered door and cascades down the apartment's front steps. A single set of wet footprints disappears down the sidewalk into the blackness.

"Jesus, water heater musta blown."

Lucy retrieves her text phone from on top of the dash and begins to beat out a quick alert to Eugene, but stops before hitting the send button.

"Maybe they've already gone for help," she thinks and continues to watch the flow and look for any movement behind the translucent curtains. But the only thing stirring is the Johnston that quivers beneath her.

Lucy hits the kill switch, clicks open the door and carefully climbs down to the sidewalk. The street is deserted with the early morning fog still hanging at treetop level. She bends to stick a pinky into the sidewalk flow and after a sniff and taste is satisfied with her original guess. At the apartment's front window, Lucy can just make out a television's flickering screen in front of an empty recliner with its seat full of blankets. A dim floor lamp stands guard next to the chair. Climbing the front steps, she thumps on the door with the palm of an open hand.

Trying to control the strength of her breathing to get the right intonation, she calls out: "Hulla, iss anyon a hoom." Lucy's out of practice since Ramon prefers that she sign or use the TTY while Eugene and the guys at the yard speak to her face and don't expect much in return.

Eugene had found Lucy one morning at the bus shelter outside of the Public Works yard, cleaning up the mess that the homeless had left from their previous night's slumber. They took her on as a temporary worker picking up trash and cleaning toilets. But her bosses soon realized that Lucy's special condition could be useful, and she's now in charge of operating the noisy Johnston and testing the emergency sirens that warn town folk of catastrophes at the nuclear power plant.

"Those damn sirens will bust an eardrum if you're on a pole when they blow," Eugene had said, and Lucy wondered how he knew this and what had become of her predecessor. But the one sound that both she and Ramon longed for had never come, had never brought joy to their home. She still dreams of swept verandas in the Mexican heat and the coarse feel of cut stone under tiny, brown feet.

Lucy thumps one more time on the apartment's front door, then reaches for the antique glass knob and gives it a healthy twist. She's surprised to find it open and hesitates before slowly pushing inside, calling out again, this time with more force.

"Anyon hoom, itss Pubic Works!"

A dark hallway disappears into the black interior with a single chevron of light cutting across it at the opening to the front room. Lucy moves forward with fists clenched, calling as she goes, knowing that at any moment a door could fly open and someone challenge her. She peeks into the living room and finds overstuffed furniture sheathed in plastic with newspapers, pizza boxes, and beer cans scattered everywhere. Opened and sealed mail litters a coffee table holding an ashtray full of crimson-tipped butts, one of them still smoking.

But the flow of water under Lucy's feet is insistent, and she ignores the clutter and pushes further into the interior, her boots slipping on the wet wooden floor until she crosses the hall and edges along its dry side.

A golden line gleams under a door at the far end, and the water seems to be flowing from that direction. She pauses to let her eyes adjust to the gloom and continues to call out, but with less force. Halfway to the light something soft brushes against her legs, and she jumps, a shout of air forced upward and out her lips. Staring down, the eyes of a huge Siamese stare back at her, mouth agape in full complaint. Trembling, Lucy pulls off a work glove and gives the cat a good scratch behind the ears, feeling the purring rumble through its body.

"*El Gato Loco*," she mutters nervously before pressing forward. At the end of the hall she bangs on the door with a closed fist. The scent of Ivory and baby powder hangs heavily in the stuffy air, making Lucy anxious to be outside, in her fan-cooled glass box gliding through the darkness. She lets her breathing slow and studies how the rivulets of water spill out from under the door; they are clear, and when she bends to them with an ungloved hand, feel cold to the touch.

"Screw this — the cops can figure it out," she thinks and turns to go, but abruptly decides otherwise and grasping the doorknob, pushes inside.

The bank of lights over the bathroom sink momentarily blinds her, but not soon enough, and she turns quickly away. A shudder like an ungrounded electric current runs through her and she slumps onto the commode to steady herself. But after a few minutes Lucy can't help but look. Over the rolled top edge of an old claw foot bathtub pours a steady curtain of clear water, splashing down onto the dirty linoleum and disappearing into the hallway. A man's naked body lies submerged in this minor lake, his open brown eyes, made huge by the water, staring up at the mildew-spotted ceiling. He is short and looks Latino or maybe Arabic and well over seventy; the grizzled, white chest hair and lined gaping face full of gold teeth give that away. Old, homemade tattoos cover his lower arms, and one leg looks withered as if from polio.

Slowly rising, Lucy inches forward and reaches behind the body to turn off the flowing taps. In a few minutes, the waterfall stops, and the man rests in peace, except for a pained facial expression that Lucy won't forget soon. There is no blood, no obvious wound, and no sign of anything violent.

Lucy pulls at the chain hooked over the spigot, and the tub slowly drains. Reaching for a towel, she drapes it over the man's private parts and leans back on the edge of the sink, giving herself time to stop trembling and fight back the urge to flee the apartment and continue her route as if nothing has happened. She's already late finishing up the West End and can do nothing for this man — besides, remembering the disappearing wet footprints, Lucy feels there's no one left to complain.

Some time passes before she leaves the bathroom, closing the door softly and retracing her steps down the hall. Glancing once more into the living room, Lucy momentarily thinks about attacking the clutter. She purposefully walks to the television and searches for the remote to turn it off. On a nearby table, a framed photograph of the old man in the tub stares back: He's wearing some kind of uniform and a toothy grin, a young rounded woman with dangerous eyes leans against him, unsmiling.

Probing the mound of blankets in the recliner as a likely location for the remote, her gloved hand hits something solid that moves. Lucy vaults backward into the TV, knocking it off its stand and nearly onto the floor. The blankets continue to move, and once again Lucy bites back the urge to get away, her heart can take only so much. Kneeling on the dirty carpet, she watches the blankets as they periodically spasm outward. Removing both work gloves, she slowly begins to pull back the top layers until a tiny face stares up at her, toothless mouth wide open, cheeks red and wet, tiny arms flailing.

"*Jesus y Maria.*"

The tiny one's eyes shift to the source of this strange new sound, and its mouth closes for a brief moment before resuming its soundless outrage. Gently, Lucy reaches in and grasping the child under the arms, hauls it up. Ignoring the wet diaper that has leaked onto the blanket, she clasps it to her breast, feeling the tiny heart beating at a squirrel's pace while she smoothes its long strands of black hair that stand straight up, tickling her chin.

After a while, the baby's eyes are half closed with tiny air bubbles forming between perfectly curved lips. A thousand and one questions race through Lucy's mind as she crouches, rocking on her heels. Gradually, she becomes aware of gray light pouring through the front window. It's *cinco y media* and she was due back at the yard a half hour ago. They'll be out looking for her soon.

As the Johnston accelerates along the boulevard, Lucy stares once again at the bouncing photographs and grins. She makes a hard right at the end of Saint Francis Avenue and pulls up in front of their home. Ramon will still be sleeping on his day off, but her new surprise should keep him busy. She wonders if they still have the information about baby monitors stored somewhere — unless it got swept away in one of Lucy's urges to clean. It would be a shame to miss seeing this little one's first words.

THE KIND OF QUIET IT IS

Fiction

Cathy Rose

It was the big ferry, the Pocahontas, and usually they all got out of the car, climbed the metal stairs to the upper deck and watched the boat cut its way across the James towards Surry, the county before Isle of Wight. And just before the ferry bounced off the pilings on the Surry side, Junie's daddy would say, it's like another world over here, another world, and she knew he meant the world of his childhood and the country people, what her daddy wasn't now, thank goodness, he said. But this morning it was windy, and Junie's mamma said no to getting out of the car and waving goodbye to one side and hello to the other. So she and her brother, Kevin, had to sit in the back and listen to her mamma and daddy. They were talking about Great Auntie Del and how they were not so happy to be going to her house for Christmas.

"Your Aunt Del just doesn't accept me," her mamma said.

"It's me she doesn't accept. I doubt she even thinks about you."

"Well, that's just as bad, John. Don't you think that's just as bad?"

They stopped then, just long enough for the Pocahontas to sound its horn at a barge out in the channel. "She accepts your brother and *he* left Isle of Wight. He lives in Richmond, for God's sake; it's three times the size of Williamsburg!" But Junie's daddy said to her mamma, they're just railroad people, Richard and Arlene, and Richard helps Aunt Del. He helped her find the man to put in the new well. Junie's mamma handed a bag of pretzels back to her, and Junie tried to pass them on to Kevin, but he had his head in a *National Geographic*.

"I can't get a conversation going with your aunt or with any of them," her mamma said. "They're not interested in your work. They glaze over when I talk about my music. Maybe I should say it's the fiddle I play!"

"They're hick but they're not hee-haw, Janice," Junie's daddy said laughing. "And there are always the children. Nobody can fault you for talking about children."

"I suppose," her mamma said, looking out her side window at the gulls bouncing in the gusty air. "But I don't want us talking about the other night with Junie. No sense adding our gruesome little kitchen incident to their Southern gossip column."

"So, honey," she said, leaning around to the back seat, "just chew your food thoroughly and everything will be fine."

Junie nodded okay, but it was not okay. And she looked over at Kevin because he had seen what had happened the other night at supper. She'd tried to tell her mamma she couldn't go to Great Auntie Del's this Christmas because how would she eat the big dinner. Since she'd choked on the piece of meat the other day, only applesauce and soup broth would go down. Her throat was broken, it *was*. But when Junie had let her dinner get cold, her mamma had gotten so mad, she wanted to spank her. "Junie, this is ridiculous," she'd said, "There is nothing wrong with your throat."

The ferry cut its engine and bobbed before it finally docked on the other shore. "They're putting a nuclear power plant over here in Surry," her daddy said, buckling back his seatbelt. "I might do some legal work for them."

"Returning to your roots, are you?" her mamma teased, because then he'd be working here on the country side of the James River.

"Hardly," he said.

"What about your teaching?"

"I can do both. Hey, I thought you wanted that house in Queen's Lake."

Then her mamma reached over and rustled her daddy's hair so he laughed. "And they said I shouldn't marry a country boy!"

Once you were in Surry County, it was still a long windy way to Isle of Wight. At least today, her daddy said, there weren't hog trucks and tractor trailers to slow up traffic. They could speed along the two-lane road, through the corn fields and peanut fields, past the falling down farmhouses, past the mobile homes, and the newer, all-alike brick ones. There were plastic Santas and reindeer on some of the roofs, and almost all the houses, even the tractors and old cars parked out in the yards were strung with bright colored Christmas lights.

Junie liked the colored lights on this side of the James because at home, they only had white lights on the tree and white candles on the window sills. Her mamma didn't like the colored, nobody in their neighborhood did, because white is more 18th Century, her mamma said, and most people in Williamsburg want to retain the old Virginia Colonial feel. *Most* people, her mamma said, because some had the colored lights in Williamsburg. Their ironing lady did.

When she choked on the meat, though, it was white lights she saw, blinking white dots, and she had heard her daddy say, step away, just let her cough it out, because her mamma had been trying everything, hitting her on the back and reaching down her throat, but nothing, not anything was working. "Cough, Junie!" her daddy had yelled, and she had tried to do what he said instead of what she heard inside, "Junie is going to heaven, to heaven, to heaven." "Cough, Junie!" he had hollered, and she had done what her daddy told her.

"Joe and Jimmy'll be at Great Auntie's, won't they?" Kevin said. kicking on the back of the front seat. Yep, their daddy nodded, and Kevin said, "Swell," because even though Joe and Jimmy's family were only railroad people, they liked to play with their cousins.

Great Auntie Del's house was old, but not, her mamma said, in a quaint way. It was too much like a box, with a sagging side porch not big enough for a swing. And it hugged the edge of the highway, which might have been okay when it was a dirt road or just a country lane, but now that Gwaltney was in Isle of Wight, and Planter's Peanuts, the road had become a thoroughfare for trucks and not something you want to live on. So they had to be careful when they played outside. Junie's mamma reminded them of that as their car pulled into Great Auntie Del's driveway.

"Lord have mercy, look at the youngens!" Aunt Martha cried as she flung the front door open.

"Nice to see you, Martha," Junie's daddy said, touching her arm lightly.

"Season's greetings, Martha," her mamma said.

Great Auntie Del's front parlor was overflowing with the country relatives all talking at once with drawls so thick it was hard for Junie to understand them. Some were Junie's aunts and uncles, her daddy had lots of brothers and sisters. And some were cousins, all grown and with their own children. And some were people only Great Auntie Del was related to. Junie knew that Great Auntie Del had turned into her daddy's mamma after his parents died, so even though she was her daddy's auntie, she was also his mother, though her daddy said it was only partly so because he was almost grown when it all happened.

"Come on here!" It was Aunt Arlene and Uncle Richard from Richmond waving them over. They always sat with them at Great Auntie Del's, because besides living in the city, Arlene and Richard weren't farmers or hog people like the country relatives, so it wasn't as hard to find things to talk about.

"How's it going at the railroad?" Junie's daddy said, shaking Uncle Richard's hand.

"Oh, still trying to make the trains run on time."

"Are Joe and Jimmy here?" Kevin said, looking around the parlor. But her mamma said, hush, Kevin, because it was rude to interrupt like that.

Great Auntie Del always wore an apron because she cooked for them all when they came at Christmas, and her apron this time had pots and pans and tea kettles on it and words that said "pots" and "pans" and "skillets" and "kettles." And when Junie read the words, she thought "kettles" is a country word like "fiddle." And she saw Great Auntie Del had on one of her house dresses, the kind that snapped up the front. Her mamma always laughed at how all the women here wore those for the Christmas dinner, and how the men's clothes were just a step up from coveralls. Their family, because her mamma said they must, dressed in their Sunday best even though it was only the country they were going to.

"The youngens is growed," Great Auntie Del said to her mamma.

"Yes, Junie's in second grade and Kevin is in fourth, and they're both doing very well."

"And how you makin' out?" Del asked Junie's daddy.

"Working hard," he said, "Things are fine."

Then they all were quiet, her daddy was so much quieter than usual, till Uncle Richard jumped in and told them all about getting the well put in for Auntie Del, how Great Auntie Del's house had always shared a well with the next door neighbors but now with the new one, Del would have her own fresh-from-the-ground drinking water.

"Tastes great, too, don't it, Del?"

"I reckon," Great Auntie Del said.

But Uncle Richard wouldn't settle for that. He said, "Oh, come now, you know it does," and then Auntie Del lifted her eyes and smiled a little at him. Great Auntie Dell liked Uncle Richard; she liked him especially.

After she left to tend to dinner, Uncle Richard told them all how Auntie Del was more happy than she seemed, that she really wanted the well because she was thinking there might come a time when she'd need to sell the house and go to the nursing home in Suffolk, only she couldn't sell the house if it didn't have its own well. Great Auntie Del was old; Junie could tell by the wrinkles. But it was hard to picture her living anywhere but in her house. And it was hard to picture Great Auntie Del dead because that's what happened to people when they went to nursing homes. Grandma Pricilla from Charlottesville had died in a nursing home. In a nice one, her mamma said.

Then Joe and Jimmy came in from outside. They *were* here, and Junie and Kevin asked if they could go play with them. But their mamma said, wait, it would be polite to visit with the grown-ups a while longer. Then they all listened in on the country relatives who were talking about what had happened to Great Auntie Del the other day. It was a funny story that made everyone laugh.

"She was settin' to defrost the Frigidaire," one of the aunts said. "She'd taken all the food out, a side of Smithfield ham, the butter beans from R.C.'s garden, a big pan of Jell-O salad she'd just done makin', but when she reached to unplug it, her arm wouldn't come out from behind it. And Auntie Del pulled and pulled, but it wasn't comin', so finally, she had to slide her fanny on the cold floor with her arm up and back a bit, and pray to Jesus, someone to save her!"

"And it was the man digging the well finally found her," a country uncle piped in. "When she heard him out front, she called, 'Mr. Poteet, help an old lady out yonder in the kitchen!' And the well man, he says when he found her on the floor, arm pinned to the back, she said, 'Walter Poteet, you get me out from behind this Frigidaire but don't you look none at my knees!' Her dress, it'd scoot up like—"

And when the uncle got to the part about Great Auntie Del's dress scooting up, everybody started laughing, and Junie's mamma and daddy were laughing, too, right along with the country relatives, and she thought maybe this year on the car ride home, they will not complain about the trip to Great Auntie Del's house. Maybe this year, they will say they had a good time at Great Auntie Del's.

When the laughing was done, no one seemed to know what to talk about next so after a while Junie's mamma volunteered that the family had gone to hear an 18th Century caroling group perform the week before, and it had been just lovely. Her mamma looked so happy as she told the story, and it had been a special evening, even Kevin had liked it. Surely, Junie thought, the country relatives will like her mamma now. But while a few of the relatives nodded, most just reached for the peanuts Auntie Dell had placed out or started talking among themselves, and Junie saw her mamma's face turn inward the way it does when she is cross.

"She played the violin for it," Junie's daddy said. But one of the country aunts changed the subject. She asked what was the emblem on Kevin's jacket, and her mamma said, and all of a sudden the whole room was listening again. "It's the emblem of the academy, the children attend a private academy in Williamsburg." And Kevin leaned over to Junie and whispered, "Nobody calls our school the academy," and Junie said, "I know." And they both wished their mamma would hush, but she went on and told them all about Kevin winning the Junior Fife and Drum Corp award and about Junie, how Junie was going to act in a children's Shakespeare troupe at the College of William and Mary.

"Ain't she shy for actin'? I never heard a word outa the child," one of the relatives said. And Junie thought, yes, I am shy, and I am also too afraid to eat the dinner that Great Auntie Del is cooking up in the kitchen, and what would she do when they sat around the dining room table. She did not want to see the blinking white lights. She did not want to choke and die. And would Auntie Del have a new pan of Jell-O made, because maybe it would go down her throat like the soup had, only maybe she would be too afraid to ask for it on her plate because she was not from the country. And Great Auntie Del did not like it if you were not from the country.

Finally her mamma told them they could go out and play, so Jimmy, Joe, Kevin, and Junie bundled up and headed out to the tracks. It was fun to hop along the wooden ties and listen by the rails for oncoming trains. But these days it was only freight trains, her daddy had told them that, and just one a day if you were lucky, not like in the old days when car loads of passengers came down from Roanoke or up from the Norfolk shipyard. "Believe it or not, this place used to be bustling," he said, like he wanted her mamma and Kevin, and Junie, too, to know it wasn't always such a backwards place, the place he was raised hadn't always been so hick.

The town's bank was long gone, but a huge safe, still locked, stood on the building's foundations, and maybe, they all thought, there was money in it. The boys found sticks and tried to pry open the safe, then threw rocks at the safe to try and crack it open. Joe pretended to be a bank robber. "Pow-pow," he said, shooting at Kevin.

"Pow-pow back," Kevin said.

"No, you're the teller, dummy, you're dead." Joe snickered at Jimmy and slouched against the safe. He was nearly as tall as it. "My daddy says your daddy should buy Great Auntie Del a self-defrostin' 'frigerator, but he won't do it 'cause he's too busy living his big shot life in Williamsburg."

"You don't know what my daddy's gonna do," Kevin said. But Junie thought, Joe is right, my daddy isn't thinking of buying Great Auntie Del a new Frigidaire. He and mamma are busy planning the new house in Queens Lake. They're talking about the new refrigerator they will buy for *it*, and about all the other things they want to get to make their lives better. "I want my boyhood in Isle of Wight, all the deprivation, those years of always going without, to be a distant memory," her daddy had said. And it wasn't just warm jackets and bicycles and lunch money her daddy didn't have back then, it was also parents, because they died, first his mamma in a wreck, and then his daddy of liquor, and so he had to have Great Auntie Del instead, and he didn't like it.

"Let's play this is Great Auntie Del's 'frigerator," Joe said. "Junie, you be Great Auntie with her arm stuck behind it. Jimmy'll be the well man and come and rescue you." Junie did what he wanted, she put her arm behind the safe like it was the Frigidaire. She pretended she was trying to unplug it to do the defrosting. "Now act like it's stuck," Joe said, grabbing onto her arm so it really was caught there. "Act like it hurts," he said, twisting it.

"Ow," Junie said, because it really did hurt, what he was doing.

"Now fall down, fall down, like Great Auntie did," he said, yanking. "And when Jimmy comes in, say, 'Mr. Poteet, get me out from behind this Frigidaire, only don't you look none at my knees!'" And when he said that, both cousins started laughing. Junie said she didn't want to, but Jimmy said do it, come on. And so Junie slid all the way down on the concrete, and Jimmy grabbed one of the sticks they'd been using to pry the safe open and starting poking her with it. Then he pulled up her dress as far as her panties.

"There," he said. "That's it." Junie's face grew hot. She tried to kick the stick and to pull her arm from Joe. But she was trapped, like Auntie Del, and much worse than just her knees was showing.

"Let her arm go," Kevin said. "Let it go!" Kevin said, threatening to sock him.

"Auntie Jean's right. You *are* too shy for actin'," Jimmy said, flinging his stick out across the open lot. I am not, Junie wanted to say. But really, she wished her mamma would not put her in the children's Shakespeare troupe at the college. She did not want to do it. But more than that she wished that Jimmy had not pulled her dress up like that. She was scared of dying, but for a minute she had wanted to. And as they walked back along the railroad tracks, Junie thought of Auntie Del with her arm pinned behind the Frigidaire, sitting on the cold kitchen floor. She had twisted her arm, she had called out for help, "Somebody please … I'm an old lady trapped, won't somebody …?" But who could hear a lone voice back in the kitchen with the noisy trucks passing on the highway. "Help an old lady, but don't you look none at my — *panties*."

When they came through the front door, they were hit with gusts of warm air from the furnace and the smell of dinner almost out of the oven. Junie and Kevin nestled in beside their mamma and daddy on the couch. It had not been fun at all with Joe and Jimmy. Junie was glad to be inside. But then Junie's mamma leaned over to say, "Now when we sit down to dinner, don't make a scene, Junie, just chew," and Junie thought, there is *nowhere* I want to be, not outside and not inside, not in Williamsburg or in Isle of Wight, not on earth and not up in heaven. She did not know what to do because dinner was almost ready.

Great Auntie Del came to the door of the parlor, "Who can help settin' the table?" And though some of the country relatives promised that in a minute they would, Junie saw that nobody went. And Junie wanted to go, she wanted to badly, to see, instead of Smithfield ham, if there would be Jell-O salad she could eat for dinner. And somehow she wanted to look at the refrigerator that had caused Auntie Del all the trouble.

"I can, I do at home," Junie said to Great Auntie Del, who huffed and looked back round into the parlor like she'd wanted someone else to volunteer, her daddy or one of the aunties.

Great Auntie Del's kitchen was big and old-fashioned with checkered counter tops, shellacked pine cabinets, and a round table and chairs like cowboys have in the movies. On the wall hung plates with painted red roosters. Near the back door, Junie saw the Frigidaire. She had never looked behind their refrigerator at home, or maybe the one they had at home wasn't anything like Great Auntie Del's. Hers was shorter and rounder at the corners, and on the backside of Great Auntie's, there were black rods crisscrossing like ribs, like the ribs of a side of meat from the butcher shop, and she did not think their refrigerator had those ribs. She hoped theirs did not have those.

"Child, what you lookin' at? Come on and help me here." Great Auntie Del lifted the Smithfield ham from the oven and placed it on the table. The ham was huge and heavy, Great Auntie flinched a little in the lifting, but she was used to its weightiness, Junie knew that. Great Auntie Del's daddy and Junie's father's daddy, too, before he died, were hog people, and you cooked hams when you were hog people, lots and lots of them. "I'd never *had* a hamburger until my freshman year at UVA," her daddy had told them all one evening when they were parked outside of Burger Chef. "Can you imagine, never having a hamburger until you're in college?"

Peeling back the foil, Great Auntie Del carved out a long thin slice of ham and laid it on a plate to cool. Junie looked down at the curvy lines that ran through the pink slice, and the bits of skin clinging to its edges. "Chew it," Junie heard her mamma say, "You must chew your food, chew it, don't be ridiculous, you are rid–ic–ulous." But the other night, she *had* chewed, and the choking had happened anyway. And her mamma hadn't been able to help. And "cough!" was all her daddy could say. Junie looked again over at the Frigidaire and hoped there was Jell-O salad in it.

Then Junie's daddy was there at the kitchen door. In his jacket and tie and hard-soled shoes, he looked funny in Great Auntie's country kitchen. "Del, we're concerned out here Junie's bothering you."

"Bothering? No, she's *helpin'*." Great Auntie sounded almost mad when she said that, mad or sad, Junie wasn't sure which, because a long time ago, her daddy had not helped. Instead of looking out for the hogs and the garden and all the younger children when their daddy had died of liquor, he'd run off to go to college. "Del was not happy," her daddy had once told them on a car ride home, "but I had to get out. The needs are never ending in Isle of Wight, and they were threatening to swallow me whole."

"Well, I can ask Janice," her daddy said, "It'd be a good way for you two to spend a little time."

"I ain't got time for spendin' time," she said.

Her daddy sighed. "Dell, I'm glad you got the well in."

"Richard got it done. Nothing more to say 'bout the well." Auntie Del shoved her blouse sleeve up to her elbow and went back to the ham.

Junie's daddy glanced back into the parlor. "Well, for the record," he said with an exasperated smile, "We've offered to help out here."

Junie watched the slices of ham fold over the knife's sharp edge until her eyes fell upon the spotted blue and yellow splotches up and down the inside of Auntie Del's arm: bruises, horrible bruises from where her arm was wedged against the coils of the Frigidaire. Had her daddy seen them? Junie turned towards the door frame, but he had joined the others in the parlor. There is nothing you can do for a bruise, her daddy had once told her. There is nothing to be done for it, he had said one day in the playground when she had banged her knee. And cough was all he could say when she had choked at the dinner table. Step away, and let her cough it out. And now Auntie Del had bruises.

Del left for the dining room to retrieve the crystal butter dish. Alone, Junie's eyes fell back on the Frigidaire. Her hand reached for its handle. "What you up to, child?" Auntie Del said, suddenly appearing at the door.

Junie froze. "I choked."

"Well then, come on and get some well water from the tap," Great Auntie Del said reaching for a glass. But Junie told her no, it was at supper the other night that it had happened, and she couldn't eat, she couldn't eat the dinner.

"Choked, what'd you choke on?"

"Gristle," Junie said.

Great Auntie shook her head and sat back down at the table. "Oh," she said, "Ain't nothing worse than gristle."

Laughter erupted out in the parlor. She heard her daddy along with all the others. "Did you think you would die, Great Auntie?"

"What in the world? What you talkin' about, child?"

"When you were stuck behind the Frigidaire?"

Auntie Del didn't answer. She reached for the paper napkins, her fingers folding them into triangles. I am wrong for what I am asking, Junie thought. Auntie Del is too busy, too busy for spendin' time. You are ridiculous, Junie, don't be rid–ic–ulous. But then Auntie Del set down the napkins. Her hands fell to her lap. "Why yes, child, I saw right many stars 'fore Mr. Poteet come. I reckon heaven *was* a calling me. But I'm all right … I'm all right now."

Then for a moment, the two sat in the kitchen, still and quiet. But it was not the kind of quiet grown-ups sometimes are when they do not know what else to say. It was more the kind that happens at night when you cannot sleep and lay your pillow by the window to see out, and your mamma and daddy are near but not near, far and near.

"Bless your heart, child," Great Auntie Del said, "Bless your heart."

Auntie Del put out the plates, tea glasses, and cups for the ambrosia, and Junie laid out the forks, knives, and spoons. Finally, the table was ready. "But one more thing," Auntie Del said. Great Auntie brought Junie to the back of the kitchen and stood with one hand on her own head and the other on top of the refrigerator. "Now see here," she said to Junie, "how big this Frigidaire is next to your Great Auntie Del, and with a motor'll outlive her to boot. But that gristle, how big was that gristle you was wrestlin'?"

Junie looked up at Great Auntie Del. She made a space of a few inches between her fingers. "All right," Del said, bringing Junie out before the hall mirror. "Now lookie here, child, how big *you* is."

When Junie's mamma and daddy came into the dining room, they were talking about how they'd need to head back pretty much right after dinner, they didn't want to miss the eight o'clock ferry because then they'd have to wait for the nine, and the children, they were too tired the whole next day if they got back too late in the evening. And Aunt Arlene said, that's why they always stayed over at Auntie Del's, that it was better to stay over so you could make a fresh start in the morning. But then they were all interrupted by Uncle Richard, because now that they were all seated, he wanted to make a toast.

"To all of us comin' here, from city, town, and country, too. And to Auntie Del and her brand-new well, sweet iced tea ne'er tasted better." Then the ham was passed around, along with butter beans, tomato pudding, and sweet baby corn, and her mamma put a little of each on Junie's plate, and washing the bites down with water, she ate it. "Well" rhymes with "Del," Junie thought. "Great Auntie Del has a well, and her well is swell."

Driving home, the highway was always pitch black, and the white stripes that ran down the center and the Christmas lights from the occasional houses on either side were their only markers. And there were deer on that road, once they had almost hit one, so every year her mamma reminded him, be careful, John, please be careful. And Junie's daddy drove fast, too fast, like he was running a race that began in Isle of Wight and ended in their driveway back home. It scared Junie, so she slept, but it was in and out, in and out, and it was the waking you remembered. This year, she woke to a blur of flashing color on a mailbox, to the sound of their tires as they rounded a turn outside of Smithfield, to the bucking of waves under the ferry's hull, and finally to white lights, delicate white lights everywhere. Was she dying? No, it was Williamsburg, and they were home. In front, her mamma and daddy were talking quietly, so quietly that she could hardly make out a word, until her mamma reached over, "John," she said, rubbing the nape of his neck, "I love our life."

CLEPSYDRA
Elizabeth Klise von Zerneck

They say it was a clear improvement
over the sundial. And while I can't speak
to the specific mechanics involved —

a float tank, a water supply,
some sort of reservoir — I do know something
about measuring time with water.

I've done it all my life: counted out
the seasons with each rainy day, filled my years
from the kettle and the tap,

calculated again and again the number of knots
needed to cross each of my various oceans.
And don't get me started

on the tears. One downside
of the clepsydra was that it could not
identify an actual hour, but only measure

a set time period. The sundial, of course,
had its own serious drawback,
since one couldn't read the time

in cloudy weather or the dark. And so
I ask you what I ask myself today — which
of these is the greater loss —

to never know the exact time, or
to be unable to measure the passing of an hour
on a day as dark as this?

STUMP, MEDFORD HILLSIDE
Brad Clompus

Our son, almost four, calls to it,
so we stand him on the pedestal's
slick crown. He wobbles,
the stump's restless ornament.
Soon he is squatting, minutely
absorbed with the progress
of a wine-dark ant. It emerges
from a crack in the bark, swigs
some air, reenters the defile.
Our son wants to know where
it went. Gone inside, I say,
to their great city and I paint
the interstitial ramps, the spirals,
arches and spiked gates we're
not allowed to see. *Make them
come out*, he says, but who can
know if that ant was just the one,
or emissary of a tribe that is bred
better than to show off their
groundling heads. I change
topics to the job of counting
rings — an incremental form
of magic I pretend to know.
Some rings are packed close,
others drifting apart, the years
of plenty and hurt occurring in no
special order. The lighter earlywood,
the darker latewood of each year
counted together, read as one.
Twice I lose track so I scout
decades, declare the tree to be
around a hundred — twice dad's
age. *Is that really, really old
or just a little old*, my son asks.
The stump rises roughly
to the plane of my belly.
My wife, a meter of logic
if it's wanted, looks down
at the rings, then to me.
It is just before or after rain,

the sky is pervasively damp,
with tattered splotches of cloud
riddling hatched panes of sky.
She counts differently,
modestly, without so much
weather. Claims it's more
like fifty. But I say you need
to look lower on the base,
where the stump thickens.
That's where they hide, that's
where you make the cut.

OPHELIA UNRAVELING
Carol Berg

Lord, we know what we are but know not what we may be.
                                   Hamlet IV. v. 42, 43

I dove once into
the wind

which swirled me

like a ruckus of apple
            blossoms falling

                not unlike Hamlet's
bed with its early mornings of satin
sadness
                I swore not
to divorce the kiss   My lips

a tight commerce

wind's wet mouth upon me

Couldn't he see

I was gulping his name
I was the pale
            shimmer

of moon-sliver
            I was glass-shard glint

surfacing the encouraging river

I   was   sky blown
                        skein

        of blue   skin

I was
                unpinned
                            by wind

INVERTED
Wendy Vardaman

It's no surprise to find my father flat
out on the ironing board —
stretched chair to floor — my mother puts him there, head
down, feet
elevated as soon as he complains about
his sad
back, ruined
by some long-ago-I-used-to-be-young sports accident,

and unresponsive, by the time he soaked-and-dried waits pressing,
to self-medication — one-fourth a carton, two
six-packs, and a half-a-fifth per day. He blinks — as home from
        seventh grade I pass his door
on tip-toe, hoping to avoid the steam — and asks me for a glass of
        something
to restore his starch — a request that I
pretend not to hear.

LUMINANCE
Wendy Vardaman

I outlasted my mother
at six, on the Saturdays we'd gather
in growing darkness, one blanket
between us, to watch, from our crushed
velvet couch, the glowing
TV, tall as an altar, deep wood gleaming.
She'd studied the movies, could recite their plots, chapter
and verse, knew the names of each glamour
queen who lit our living
room till midnight — one — two — me mirroring
every gesture: Eyes wide,
palms pressed,
chin-lift to express devotion;
brows knit, hands-hip, determination;
back turned, fingers laced, face lowered to hide a glittering tear,
despair. I hadn't the faintest glimmer
then that my heavy-lidded, hands-limp
mother kept a vigil for my father's headlamps,
or how she must have felt
when, every station having ceased
transmission, she turned down the volume and waved
me, her pale skin glistening, to bed.

IF MY HAND TREMBLES, LET A FALCON REST UPON IT
Tayve Neese

Talons will steady my shake and sway.
If my tongue stutters, words trapped

like small bees, the raptor
will take flight, bring bloodied

backs of grouse for roasting
until my mouth is warmed,

made strong enough to say
the most brutal thing in a whisper

as soft as speckled feathers.
And if the bird does not startle from speech,

if brown and gold wings do not spread,
then I am grateful for what does not lift,

what holds tighter, claws piercing skin.

EVERYTHING RAVAGED, EVERYTHING BURNED
By Wells Tower
238 pp. Farrar, Strauss and Giroux
Hardcover. $24

It's clear from the first line of the first story in Wells Tower's collection, *Everything Ravaged, Everything Burned*, that the author not only knows how to spin a great yarn, he enjoys doing so. "Bob Munroe woke up on his face," begins the story "The Brown Coast." "His jaw hurt and morning birds were yelling and there was real discomfort in his underpants."

Wells reproduces a world of struggles, of tremendous conflicts — between characters, between people and their imaginations — but he never forgets that human beings, whatever their predicament, always seem to be able to see the absurdities, the humor of life. It's what gives his potentially depressing stories an edgy and entertaining aspect, somewhat like watching incidents on a reality show. Even Tower's photo adds to the effect — he displays a sort of impish countenance, as though he knows his stories are going to absorb and charm. They really can't help but do so —Tower's craft is as practiced and polished as any short story writer in the genre today. The language of each story is beautifully matched to the subject; simile and metaphor are first-rate.

For example, "Door in Your Eye," is the story of an old man, a war veteran, who believes the woman who lives across the street is a prostitute. Having never been with such a woman, he searches for an excuse to go to her place. Tower's accuracy in visualizing and communicating how such people would act and sound is one of the great attractions of his writing:

> My breathing was the loudest thing in the room I didn't feel steady. "Could I sit down here?" I asked her. "Could I sit on your bed?"
>
> "I don't mind."
>
> "What's your name, miss?" I couldn't hear over my heart.
>
> She stroked her throat with her fingers and took me in through half-closed eyes. "Carol," she finally said.
>
> I reached out put my water glass on the table. My hand was shaking so it made a loud noise when I set

it down.

"That's a pretty name," I said, though I didn't particularly think it was.

"Thanks," she said. I could see that under her shirt, she wasn't wearing a brassiere.

"Okay, Carol. What if you were just to get down here next to me? I just want us to lie here for a little while. What would be the price for that?"

And then there are the premises themselves. No paeans to dying, or anguished relationship issues here. Instead we have brothers, one successful, one not, vying for fraternal supremacy and the friendship of the local handyman ("Retreat"). We have the outcast boy who fears both his distant stepfather and rumors of a leopard skulking in the nearby woods ("Leopard"). We have the case of child rape at the county fair where virtually every male employee could be — and should be — a suspect ("On the Show"). The topper, the strangest, the quirkiest of them all is the title cut, "Everything Ravaged, Everything Burned." Think Vikings. Think plunder, pillage, fraternities and the gentle, unforeseen decline into middle age.

It's terribly inventive stuff, and shows a mind at work and play simultaneously, producing stories that have locomotive-like momentum — they're impossible to stop. Don't get the wrong idea, though. Tower is a hard-working and dedicated writer who goes through many drafts to get his stories right. Many of the pieces in this book have been rewritten even though they have been published previously in literary journals.

In interviews Tower says his work tends to show the darker side of human nature, that people have desires but tend to mask them in the interest of their own personal public relations efforts — in other words, people are basically hypocrites, and it shows, and in these stories it makes for good reading.

——

Joe Ponepinto's work has been published recently in *The Summerset Review*, *Raven Chronicles*, and *Los Angeles Review*. He lives in Troy, Michigan. His blog is at http://otnipenop.com.

THE VAGRANTS
By Yiyun Li
337 pp. Random House
Hardcover. $25

When the Communist government in China dabbled in the concept of free speech in the late 1970s, the idea proved popular with the masses. So popular, in fact, that as totalitarian regimes are wont to do, they soon realized the public's pent-up anger towards their leaders and shut the enterprise down, violently, in a matter of days. Yiyun Li writes of those times, when many people balanced fear and self-preservation against the idea of open discussion and a desire to throw off the burden of decades of conformity to the party line.

The Vagrants follows a cross-section of the residents of Muddy River, a city in the Chinese frontier, a former trading post where the only chance of advancement is through service to the party, and where the wrong word or impression can mean anything from loss of a job to imprisonment. Through the lives of these people, each already something of an outcast from the community, Li portrays the realities of life under a government still too new and paranoid to tolerate criticism, or even differences of opinion. That mindset is summed up beautifully in Teacher Gu — the book opens as he and his wife awaken to the day their counterrevolutionary daughter, Shan, a former supporter of the party, is scheduled to be publicly denounced and executed for speaking out against the state. While Mrs. Gu rails against the harsh punishment and makes a public demonstration to prepare her daughter for the next life, Teacher Gu has already accepted the regime's pronouncement and is in the process of rationalizing her death, erasing her memory from his mind — so conditioned is he to accept the dictates of the government. There was once, we learn later, a glimmer of his daughter's spirit in Teacher Gu. Shan's death, and the actions of the Muddy River underground rekindle those feelings in him, but even as he rediscovers his desire for freedom of thought, he restricts his opposition to secret letters written to his first wife. He is too old and sick — even after Mrs. Gu is taken away by the police in the middle of the night — still too afraid to speak his beliefs publicly.

But the most interesting of Li's "vagrants" is Wu Kai. She is the city's official announcer, speaking daily over the radio from the Department of Propaganda, and she is also the story's link to the underground movement. Dissatisfied with her life and yearning for the freedom the opposition seems to offer, she keeps her involvement with them secret, even from her husband, a low-ranking official in the party, until a public demonstration against the government's execution of Shan.

Most of the others Li depicts in her story, from children to seniors, become involved in the demonstration not so much because of political fervor, but through curiosity over the mere possibility the regime will even allow such an event. Word comes from Beijing that a "democracy wall" has been erected where people can post their questions and criticisms, which makes participation in the local public display seem, if not sanctioned, at least worth a try. Here is where Li is at her best, reminding us how most people balance personal risk against their ideals.

It's the intricacies of her characters' lives, delivered in simple, clear prose that allows Li to recreate a world that would be completely alien for most Americans, for whom criticism of the government is part of the everyday. The actions of these people are clouded by the regime. They must ponder every time they attempt anything out of the social norms dictated from Beijing: Who will see? Who will talk? Who hopes to gain from my misfortune? By linking the oppression of the times directly to the individuals who are oppressed, and presenting it in stark terms that reflect the setting and culture, Li connects our traditional expectations of freedom to the budding hopes of the people of Muddy River. When the government reacts to quash those dreams, we experience their fear and desperation, emotions made even more profound through the western perspective Li expertly and subtly infuses into her narrative.

Joe Ponepinto's work has been published recently in *The Summerset Review, Raven Chronicles,* and *Los Angeles Review.* He lives in Troy, Michigan. His blog is at http://otnipenop.com.

GRAYWOLF PRESS

John Bradley

LETTERS TO A STRANGER

By Thomas James
108 pp. Graywolf Press
Paper. $15

In 1973, a first collection of poems entitled *Letters to a Stranger* was published to little notice. Shortly after, the author, Thomas James, took his life. He was twenty-seven, and copies of *Letters* soon disappeared.

The story might have ended there but for an odd happenstance. For more than thirty years, some poets photocopied the book and pressed friends and students to read it. In 2008, Graywolf republished the book as part of its Re/View series with an extensive introduction by Lucie Brock-Broido (one of the mad photocopiers) and a section of "uncollected poems." Mark Doty, who chose James' book for the series, made an inspired choice.

Yes, the poetry has its weaknesses. The first poem, "Waking Up," uses the words "dark" or darkness" five times, evidence of the influence of Deep Image poetry on James. An even stronger influence was Sylvia Plath, her poetics as well as her infatuation with death. The title of one of James's poems, "Longing for Death," clearly demonstrates this obsession. There's even a chilling poem called "Suicide" in the "Uncollected" section.

Despite these caveats, the poetry remains compelling. James transcends his influences, something rare for a young poet's first book. For example, Lucie Brock-Broido observes that Plath's "Lady Lazarus" may have inspired James' "Mummy of a Lady Named Jemutesonekh XXI Dynasty." While this could very likely be true, James' persona doesn't confront our role as voyeurs, as does Plath. Instead we hear the quiet, disturbing voice of a woman celebrating her mummification:

> They slit my toes; a razor gashed my fingertips.
> Stitched shut at last, my limbs were chaste and valuable,
> Stuffed with paste of cloves and wild honey.
> My eyes were empty, so they filled them up,
> Inserting little nuggets of obsidian.
> A basalt scarab wedged between my breasts
> Replaced the tinny music of my heart.

While she sees what she has gained due to the art of mummification, we also see what she has lost. Her heart may have issued "tinny music," yet a stone scarab hardly offers the heart's life force. At the same time, we recognize the loss of a beating heart is part of her sacrifice for immortality. That the poem questions this sacrifice in the last line — Why do people lie to one another?" — only adds to the poem's poignancy.

Given the presence of death breathing throughout this book, readers will turn to "Suicide" looking for some answers. This poem, however, leaves us with only more questions. It opens in a cool, matter-of-fact matter that only heightens the overall emotional impact:

> Before I felt the bullet
> Nip through my brain,
> I stepped back, stepped back
> To my grandmother's house
> In the middle of summer.

Does his grandmother's "sagging porch" imply a weariness with the corruptibility of the flesh? Are we to take the lines "The flies were humming a tiny mass / For a cricket who had died" as ironic? Or a wry comment on the afterlife? Is suicide encouraged by the clock he hears whisper "*There is only a delicate hunching / Into your private death*"? (This line is in italics in the poem.) Or might suicide be the only way for the speaker to find his "other self, / the gentle one," who he comes upon in the attic of his grandmother's house? The short poem startles in the last line as the speaker's death seems to come from someone else, someone who has taken the narrator's life without reason or warning: "And then somebody slammed the attic door." By omitting exposition, James leaves us only with the chilling emotional experience of the suicide.

Mystery, as well as mortality, haunts these poems. In "The Turn of the Screw," James asks: "*Is it decay I want?*" (Italics in the original.) Here we see what tortures so many of the personas in this book. If mortality offers only decay, then why linger in the flesh? Art may be the only way of preserving something of our lives, as Lady Jemutesonekh tries to believe.

The fact that Thomas James practiced his craft as if it had life and death implications, as if this book were his letter to readers "ages hence," as Whitman said, this might explain why so many readers refused to let *Letters to a Stranger* die. We owe them, as well as Graywolf Press, much gratitude.

John Bradley teaches at Northern Illinois University and was guest poetry editor of *Fifth Wednesday Journal*'s third issue. He is the author of *Terrestrial Music* (Curbstone Press).

MILKWEED EDITIONS

Chris Fink

DRIFTLESS
By David Rhodes
352 pp. Milkweed Editions
Paper. $16

David Rhodes' *Driftless* ripens slowly, like the summer morning we meet July Montgomery as he spots a black panther slinking like the fog into a shady coulee of imaginary Thistlewaite County in the driftless region of Southwestern Wisconsin. Formerly a drifter (and holdover from Rhodes' earlier novel, *Rock Island Line*), July has found a home in the tiny hamlet of Words, Wisconsin, where he milks a small herd.

With a large cast of primary actors — July's only family, the residents of Words — Rhodes has a lot of introductions to make. Chapter by brief chapter, we meet the folks we might expect to see at a small-town church social. There's the pastor, Winnie Smith; two religious spinster sisters, Violet and Olivia Brasso; a young farm couple, the Shotwells, and an old farm couple, the Smiths; a struggling musician, also a Shotwell; a mechanic, Jacob Helm; and a heavily pierced parolee, aptly named Dale Armbuster. Stalking the weedy fringes of the novel is a group of threatening militants, and at the other end of the political spectrum, the handy, helpful Amish.

While July is the main character here, it takes the reader awhile to hunker down with this book and realize it's his story. July drifts in and out of the first half of the seventy short chapters like the secretive panther. We find July always willing to lend a hand or an ear to his neighbors but never forthcoming with his own story. It's interesting that July isn't really at the center of any of the book's conflicts. As a device he is, like the panther, more of an organizing principal. As a character he's the head of the book's household, and his role in the book is to aid his children, to help *see them through* the book, if you will. His moral compass is aligned somewhere between the author's and the reader's.

July seems to have a hand in each one of the dramas that unfold in *Driftless* — political dramas on a grand scale, like the Shotwells' battle with Big Milk, and personal crises like Olivia Brasso's "theodyssey" at the local tribal casino or Gail Shotwell's attempt finally to make her own music.

Rhodes orchestrates a satisfying and skillfully plotted array of human drama. The unfolding events are inventive and surprising, stretching the elasticity of disbelief, but not quite beyond the pale. The reader might ask, as I did, why a black panther, of all unlikely creatures? Or, when paroled Armbuster asks the disabled Brasso for a first date at a local dogfighting ring, and when she accepts, we warily accept this unlikely occurrence, but we make a note that the payoff had better be good. For the record, Rhodes comes through. The expertly delivered dogfight in *Driftless* is one of the book's signature scenes. Rhodes later does himself one better when he takes us mushroom hunting with Pastor Winnie. That scene made me want to dust off my Hamlin Garland to see if he had ever ventured to treat one of Wisconsin's time-honored spring rituals.

What's *Driftless* about? Loneliness, for one. The importance of community. Loss of spirit and subsequent recovery. To be sure, the crisis each resident of Words must overcome is at its core a crisis of spirit.

Stylistically, *Driftless* is a throwback, and Rhodes is a descendant of Garland. His distant third person narrator reports from the characters' perspective in each chapter, but he also leisurely reports theology, natural history, and philosophy. Sometimes I wished Rhodes would stay closer to his characters, for it was usually when his intonation was authorial that I found myself doubting him. I also noticed this happened more often early in the book; I second-guessed some of the choices Rhodes made, and some of the writing itself. But Rhodes won me over — either he settled into the book or I did — and by the time I reached the middle parts, I was enjoying the ride.

Religion plays a big part of this book, a little bigger part than I'd like. But then again, in most small towns I know, religion plays a little bigger part than I'd like. *Driftless* is also a peculiarly chaste book — the conception of the young panther even seems to be immaculate — and these two details in concert sometimes made me wonder what the author was up to.

But I forgave him. Rhodes main accomplishment is a thoroughly imagined and artfully rendered novel. A triumph. Other sons and daughters of the Middle Border, like myself, will see many things they recognize in these pages, and more urban readers will see many things they miss.

Chris Fink teaches English at Beloit College and edits the *Beloit Fiction Journal*. A fiction writer, many of his stories are set in his native Wisconsin.

TOMORROW'S LIVING ROOM: POEMS
By Jason Whitmarsh
78 pp. Utah State University Press
Hardcover. $19.95

Upon my first reading of Jason Whitmarsh's debut collection of poems *Tomorrow's Living Room*, winner of the 2009 May Swenson Poetry award, I was skeptical of the seemingly simple humor in some of the poems, especially in "Administration": "Richard B. Cheney / is considered brainy / because, Christ, what else is there? / A chest of old bones and foul air?" At first the simple lines, the simple diction, and the simple rhyme scheme surprisingly annoyed me, even knowing full well it was a clerihew.

After several more reads I was surprised again and again — in the best possible ways.

Whitmarsh uses form — be it metrical, inherited, or open — to propel the poems in this collection beyond the seemingly simple into a sometimes surreal world of twists, turns, humor, self-deprecation, and, most of all, surprise. It is because of the use of forms that the poems are free to be inventive and original. One prose poem in particular helped me see beneath the surface of what one, at times, could call silliness to the profound darkness of human existence Whitmarsh captures. "Two, Couchbound," for example, has the traits of a mathematical word problem: "Two's calculation of death over time: Ten thousand bodies a thousand years ago is five hundred bodies when Columbus lands..." But the chain of deathly events that occurs in the poem leads the reader from ten thousand to one: "One comes home, briefcase in hand, sobbing." The use of the prose poem form allows "Two, Couchbound" to be seemingly absurd, quick in wit, and dark in humor, but the prose poem's ability to turn quickly lets the visceral experience rupture in the end lines. Additionally, Whitmarsh's intelligently witty word play breathed life into many of the poems, such as "Change": "Change makes news / not with what's new / but by pulling / what's lost into view." The repetition and the multiple meanings of "new" add various layers to an outwardly simple poem that merits rereadings and allows for many thought-provoking interpretations.

The most brilliant aspect of this collection, and the one surprise that delighted me the most, was the narrative arc. Every poem in this collection is somehow — no matter how obvious or imagined — connected to every other one. The manuscript is so perfectly woven that no thread was left to fray; all the pieces unite into multiple messages and meanings that allow different readers to get something unique from his or her reading experience. The poem "Why Poetry? Because" draws attention to the narrative arc: "I can't write a novel, said the raised hand. / I'm too dramatic, it takes lots of work…" A couple stanzas later the narrator claims, "I think it's better to stick to what I know, / which is me, or the parts I've seen so far." In a sense, this collection is a narrative of the "parts … seen so far;" it's self-aware of its narrative, as seen in the poem "The Story You're Telling": "I don't mind the story you're telling, but can you please lean back in the chair and turn the light down." What finally made me laugh out loud was this awareness of narrative and how the poems in this collection (and poems in general) are not narratives like those we expect from novels. Essentially, Whitmarsh is toying — in the most fun way — with the readers' expectations of narrative(s). To illustrate, one of the collection's narratives is the "Anniversary" poem series, which follows the demise of a married couple. One of the "Anniversary" poems begins, "We number our fights and say the numbers instead of the saying the words." This beginning line immediately evokes the parents fighting in the car in the poem "Nightmare," an emotionally electric poem about a son who isn't scared of "the closet with its vast unseen / collection of unhappy monsters," but is scared of his parents' "front-seat attacks, our bedridden fights, / our blank, scarred days." The last line from "Anniversary" echoes the sentiment, in "Nightmare," of protecting children from parental fights: "I have one, too, a number and a packed bag and the children to think of." The beauty of this manuscript is that there are narrative arcs and dialogues between the poems, and these are strengthened by the fact that the collection is not divided into sections. Because there are no sections a reader is encouraged to pause after a poem and recall the other poems that feel "related" to it. In short, the interconnectedness of this collection and its narrative arcs enrich each reading.

And after every reread of *Tomorrow's Living Room* one thing becomes clear: Whitmarsh is a poet worth keeping an eye on.

Amanda McGuire regularly reviews poetry for *Fifth Wednesday Journal*. Her own poems have appeared recently in the *Cream City Review*, *NOON: Journal of the Short Poem*, and *27 rue de fleures*. She is the featured editor of the Food and Wine segment for Connotations Press. Amanda lives in Bowling Green, Ohio.

CONTRIBUTORS

J.R. ANGELELLA is a regular contributor to *The Chapbook Review*, and his short fiction has been published in *Twelve Stories*, *Word Riot*, *The Literary Review*, and *Hunger Mountain*. He lives in Brooklyn with his wife, Kate, and is at work on his first novel about adolescence, adults, and amputations. He received an M.F.A. in Writing from the Bennington Writing Seminars at Bennington College.

JACKIE BARTLEY'S poems have appeared most recently in *Harpur Palate*, *Southern Humanities Review*, and *sou'wester*. Her second poetry collection, *Ordinary Time*, won the 2006 Spire Press Poetry Prize. She is seeking a publisher for a third collection, *Sleeping with a Geologist*, and lives in Michigan with her husband John (the aforementioned geologist).

CAROL BERG has published poems in *Pebble Lake Review*, *Rhino*, *Tattoo Highway*, *Sweet*, and elsewhere. She received her M.F.A. from Stonecoast and has an M.A. in English Literature. She is a writing tutor at Pine Manor College in Massachusetts.

STEPHEN BERG is the author of numerous collections of poetry and translations, most recently *Cuckoo's Blood* (Copper Canyon Press, 2008). He has been awarded the Frank O'Hara Memorial Prize, a Columbia University Translation Prize, and fellowships from the Guggenheim, Pew, and Rockefeller Foundations, as well as from the National Endowment for the Arts. He is the founder and co-editor of *The American Poetry Review* and is professor of humanities at University of the Arts in Philadelphia.

BRAD CLOMPUS is the author of *Trailing It Home* (Main Street Rag Publishing Company, 2007) and *Talk at Large* (Finishing Line Press, 2008). His poetry and essays have appeared in *Natural Bridge*, *The Journal*, *Tampa Review*, *Tar River Poetry*, *The New Renaissance*, *Valparaiso Poetry Review* (forthcoming), and other journals. He lives in the Boston area, teaching at the Tufts University Osher Lifelong Learning Institute and the Arlington Center for the Arts.

SAMIRA GRACE DIDOS won the 2007 Gwendolyn Brooks Poetry Award sponsored by the Illinois Center for the Book. Her poetry also appears in *Poetry Miscellany* published by the University of Tennessee at Chattanooga. She is a licensed clinical psychologist in private practice. She is a graduate of the American University of Beirut and the University of Wisconsin at Madison. She has made homes in Asia, Europe, Africa, and lives in Champaign, IL.

BECKY EAGLETON is a former dancer and choreographer living in Tulsa. When her knees gave out, she returned to writing, an equally lucrative career choice. Her short stories and a novel have won or placed in various local, regional, and national competitions. Her story, "The Guy for That," will appear in the fall 2009 issue of *Blood Lotus Journal*. She just got an agent and is working on her fourth novel.

JOEL FISHBANE'S fiction can be found in back issues of *Descant, Versal, On Spec, The Antigonish Review, The Danforth Review*, and *Geist*. He has a diabetic clarinet and sometimes plays the cat.

PETRA FORD grew up in Glen Ellyn, IL., where she discovered her passion for photography. She earned a B.A. in Communication Arts from Benedictine University in 2003. Her work has recently been shown at Calmer House Gallery in Joliet, MaNa Gallery in Chicago, and Wings Gallery and Gahlberg Gallery, both in Glen Ellyn. Her photographs can be seen in the spring 2008 editions of *Fifth Wednesday Journal* and *Prairie Light Review*. Petra especially enjoys making photographs of people and the emotions, humor, and ironies that surround us. She is enrolled in photography classes at College of DuPage and lives in Wheaton, IL, with her husband and son.

AMANDA GAHLER is a junior at Wartburg College in Iowa, majoring in Communication Design and is fostering her new found passion for photography. Her favorite colors are orange, pink, and purple. She loves putting her own unique twist on everyday things and enjoys being barefoot. This year she will find herself occupied with the campus newspaper, communication and marketing department, yearbook, and online media site as a photographer.

CHRIS HAYES was awarded the 2009 Erskine J. Poetry Prize from *Smartish Pace*. His work also has been a finalist for an AWP Intro. Journals Award and was nominated for a Pushcart Prize. Forthcoming work can be found in *Zone 3, Fourth River*, and *The Country Dog Review*. He is a recent graduate of the M.F.A. program at the University of Mississippi.

JOHN KNOEPFLE has written twenty-seven books, mostly poetry. His most recent are *prayer against famine and other irish poems*, 2004; and *walking in snow* and *I Look Around For My Life: An Autobiography*, both published in 2008. Although Knoepfle has lived in the Midwest all his life and often writes about local people and places, his poetry also is concerned with global struggles and how people relate to a changing world in trying times. Right now he is writing a series of poems about the world he sees from his window. He lives with his wife, Peggy, in Springfield, IL.

THOMAS KRAPAUSKY studied photography in the Bachelor's of Fine Arts program at the University of Arkansas. He has received multiple awards locally and internationally. His work has been shown in juried exhibitions and has been published on an international level. Thomas' photos can be found in private collections across the United States and in Europe. He resides in the foothills of the Ozark Mountains in Arkansas with his wife and son.

MARK LIEBENOW's poetry has recently appeared or is forthcoming in *The Spoon River Review* and *Clackamas Literary Review*, and was nominated for an Illinois Arts Council Award. The author of three nonfiction books, he writes about hiking in Yosemite and grief recovery. He also has written about the theology of clowning and teaching the mentally challenged. He studied creative writing at the University of Wisconsin and at Bradley University.

JONATHAN LIEBSON is the author of the novel *A Body at Rest* (River City Publishing, 2010), and his stories and reviews have previously appeared in *Chelsea*, *Meridian*, *Passages North*, *Pleiades*, and *Georgia Review*, among others. He teaches writing and literature at The New School and at N.Y.U.'s School of Continuing and Professional Studies, and he can be visited at his website: jonathanliebson.com.

LISA LOCASCIO was born in 1984 and raised in River Forest, IL. She recently completed her first novel, *Peculiar Qualifications*, which is set in the suburbs of Chicago. Lisa's writing has also appeared in *The Northwest Review*, *Joyland Chicago*, *The Minetta Review*, *Prairie Margins*, and *Lake Effect*. She holds an M.F.A. in Fiction from New York University and is Virginia B. Middleton fellow at the University of Southern California's Ph.D. program in Literature and Creative Writing.

ALISON MANDAVILLE's poems have appeared in *The Seattle Review*, *13th Moon*, *The Berkeley Poetry Review*, *Poets Against the War/Best Poems*, and *Knock* among other places. Her interview with Azerbaijani author Afaq Masud appears in the September 2009 issue of *World Literature Today*. Current projects include poetry and nonfiction emerging from a recent Fulbright year in Azerbaijan. She lives in Seattle and teaches writing, literature (including comics) and women's studies at Pacific Lutheran University.

RYAN MECKLENBURG recently graduated with his M.F.A. in creative writing from The Bennington Writing Seminars. He lives in Hesperia, CA., where he works as a forklift driver in a warehouse. His other work is forthcoming. Where? He has no idea. He is at work on a collection of short stories and a novel about The Harvey-Johnson Pickle Co. Most of his free time is spent thinking about that book about a pickle company and teasing his wife, Trinity, who often deserves it.

ROBERT NAZARENE is founding editor of *Margie/The American Journal of Poetry* and *IntuiT House Poetry Series*, publishers of the 2006 winner of the National Book Critics Circle award in poetry. His volume of poems is *CHURCH*. His work has appeared in *AGNI, Callaloo, JAMA, North American Review, Ploughshares, Prairie Schooner*, and elsewhere. He divides his time between rocks and hard places.

TAYVE NEESE's poetry has appeared or is forthcoming in the following journals: *The Paris Review, caesura, The Comstock Review, Fourteen Hills, MiPoesias, The Pedestal Magazine*, and other journals. She teaches poetry at the University of North Florida and lives on Amelia Island.

DONNA PUCCIANI has published widely in the U.S. and U.K. Her poetry has appeared in such diverse journals as *International Poetry Review, National Catholic Reporter, Spoon River, Iota*, and *JAMA*. She has won poetry awards from the Illinois Arts Council, the National Federation of State Poetry Societies, and Chicago Poets & Patrons, and has been nominated twice for the Pushcart Prize. Her books include *The Other Side of Thunder, Chasing the Saints*, and *Jumping Off the Train*. The poem "Inheritance" is part of a forthcoming manuscript on her Italian heritage.

CATHY ROSE's short fiction has appeared in *Rosebud, Santa Clara Review, Fourteen Hills*, in an anthology entitled *Nixon Under the Bodhi Tree and Other Works of Buddhist Fiction*, and elsewhere. Originally from Virginia, she now resides in San Francisco where she works as a psychologist in private practice. She received her M.F.A. in creative writing from San Francisco State University.

TERRY SANVILLE lives in San Luis Obispo, CA. with his artist-poet wife (his in-house editor) and one fat cat. He writes full time, producing short stories, essays, poems, an occasional play, and novels. Since 2005, his short stories have been accepted by more than eighty-five literary and commercial journals, magazines, and anthologies including the *Houston Literary Review*, *Birmingham Arts Journal*, *Boston Literary Magazine*, and *Underground Voices*. Terry is a retired urban planner and an accomplished jazz and blues guitarist — who once played with a symphony orchestra backing up jazz legend George Shearing.

LAUREN SCHMIDT's work may be found or is forthcoming in *New York Quarterly*, *Rattle*, *Nimrod*, *Audemus*, *Slab*, and *Ruminate*. Her poems have been selected as finalists for the 2008 and 2009 Janet B. McCabe Poetry Prize and the 2009 Pablo Neruda Prize for Poetry. Originally a New Jersey native, Lauren lives and teaches high school English and Art History in Eugene, OR.

KAREN SCHUBERT's chapbook is *The Geography of Lost Houses* (Pudding House). Her poems have appeared or are forthcoming in *Zoland Poetry*, *Redactions*, *Reconfigurations*, *42opus*, and *Slant*. She received nominations for a Pushcart Prize and *Best of the Net Anthology*, and awards from American Academy of Poets and A Center for the Arts. Recent visiting writer at Texas A&M in Commerce, she serves as poetry editor for *Whiskey Island Magazine*.

PETER SERCHUK's poems have appeared in a variety of journals big and small including *Boulevard*, *Poetry*, *Denver Quarterly*, *North American Review*, *Texas Review*, *South Carolina Review*, *MARGIE* and others. Additionally, a number if his poems have been anthologized, most recently in *Against Agamemnon: War Poetry* (WaterWood Press, 2009) and *The Best American Erotic Poems 1800 to the Present* (Scribners, 2008). He has new work forthcoming in *New York Quarterly* and *North American Review*. He lives in Los Angeles.

ROB SHORE is a documentary filmmaker and photo hobbyist. His photography has been published in *Fifth Wednesday Journal*. His essays have been published by Harvard University Press and in the *Peace Corps at 50 Anniversary Story Project*. His photography, essays, and poetry have been featured on *The Best American Poetry Blog*. He graduated from Emory University in 2006 with degrees in anthropology and film. Rob currently lives in Atlanta.

ROBIN SILBERGLEID is the author of the chapbook *Pas de Deux: Prose and Other Poems* (Basilisk 2006). Her poems and essays have appeared widely in journals including *Crab Orchard Review*,

Dislocate, and *The Cream City Review*, for which she was nominated for a Pushcart Prize. She grew up in Glen Ellyn, IL, and now resides in East Lansing, MI, where she is an assistant professor of English at Michigan State University.

DAVE SMITH's recent books are *Hunting Men: Reflections on a Life in Poetry* (LSU, 2006); *Little Boats, Unsalvaged* (LSU, 2005), and *The Wick of Memory: New and Selected Poems 1970-2000* (LSU, 2000). He has edited with Robert DeMott *Afield: Writers and Bird Dogs* which is forthcoming from Skyhorse Press. He is the Elliot Coleman Professor of Poetry and Chairman of the Writing Seminars Department at Johns Hopkins University.

KRISTEN SPICKARD is a senior at the University of Central Arkansas, pursuing a B.F.A. in studio art with an emphasis in photography. She is co-director of the Black Box Student Gallery, a space which hosts twelve exhibits per year, featuring only student-made art. She recently exhibited photography in shows at Georgia University and State College and the New York Graduate School of Psychoanalysis.

ELIZABETH STROUT's most recent work, *Olive Kitteridge*, a novel in stories, won the 2009 Pulitzer Prize, was nominated for the National Book Critics Circle Award, and was a New York Times bestseller. She is the author of two previous novels, *Abide With Me*, a national bestseller, and *Amy and Isabelle*, also a New York Times bestseller, which won the Los Angeles Times Award for First Fiction, The Chicago Tribune's Heartland Prize, and was short-listed for The PEN/Faulkner Award, as well as The Orange Prize in England. Her stories have appeared in a number of magazines, including *The New Yorker*, *"O,"* and also in *Best American Mystery Stories*. She is on the faculty of the low-residency M.F.A. program at Queens College in Charlotte, N.C., and makes her home in New York City.

A.N. TEIBE's poetry and fiction have appeared in *The Pacific Review*, *Muse, Ekphrasis*, and the anthologies *Separation* and *Metamorphoses*. She makes her home in Southern California's Inland Empire where she teaches yoga and is currently a graduate student.

MAXWELL TEITEL-PAULE hides in libraries and reads dead languages. As a graduate student in Greek and Latin, he teaches, reads, writes, house-sits, snaps photos of the unsuspecting, and dances for pennies on Wednesday evenings; all he really wants for Christmas is a finished dissertation.

STEPHEN THOMAS is a retired lawyer in Chicago. He attended the University of Illinois (B.A. 1959), Harvard Law School (LL.B 1962) and the University of Chicago (M.L.A. 2008). He is a past president of the Chicago Literary Club. When not writing or doing research in 19th and early 20th Century literature and history, he may be found walking in the woods or playing jazz piano.

STEVE TOMPKINS is a graduate of Colorado State University in Pueblo and works as the director of the English Language Program at a charter school in Colorado Springs. Recent work has appeared or is forthcoming in *Big Muddy, Borderlands, Chiron Review, Cutthroat, Jelly Bucket, Natural Bridge, Nerve Cowboy*, and *New South*.

MICHAEL VAN WALLEGHEN is the author of six books of poetry, the most recent of which is *In the Black Window: Poems New and Selected* (2004). He has a Borestone Poetry Award and a Pushcart Prize. His second book, *More Trouble with the Obvious* (1981), was the Lamont Poetry Selection of the Academy of American Poets. His other books are *The Wichita Poems* (1975), *Blue Tango* (1989), *Tall Birds Stalking* (1994), and *The Last Neanderthal* (1999). He has been the recipient of two National Endowment of the Arts fellowships and several grants from the Illinois Arts Council. He is retired from the University of Illinois at Urbana-Champaign.

WENDY VARDAMAN is co-editor of *Verse Wisconsin*, her poems, reviews, and interviews have appeared in a variety of anthologies and journals, including *Poetry Daily, Breathe: 101 Contemporary Odes, Riffing on Strings, Poet Lore, qarrtsiluni, Mezzo Cammin, Nerve Cowboy, Free Verse, Women's Review of Books*, and *Rain Taxi Review*. The author of *Obstructed View* (Fireweed Press, 2009), she lives in Madison, WI, where she works for a children's theater, The Young Shakespeare Players. She has a Ph.D. in English from University of Pennsylvania

JEREMY VOIGT's chapbook *Neither Rising nor Falling* is forthcoming August 2009 from Finishing Line Press. He has poems published in *Beloit Poetry Journal, Willow Springs, Washington Square, Talking River Review*, and *REED*.

ELIZABETH KLISE VON ZERNECK's poems have appeared or are forthcoming in *Cincinnati Review, Crab Orchard Review, Measure, New York Quarterly, Ninth Letter, Notre Dame Review, The Pinch, Potomac Review, Rattle, Spoon River Poetry Review*, and *Water-Stone Review*. Her recent work was honored with the 2008 Robert Frost

Foundation Poetry Award, a 2008 International Publication Prize from Atlanta Review, and a 2009 Illinois Arts Council Fellowship Award in Poetry.

ANN WALTERS is a poet living in the Pacific Northwest. Her poems have been published or are forthcoming in *The Feathertale Review* (Canada), *The Aurorean, Folio, The Interpreter's House* (U.K.), *Carousel* (Canada), and many others. She has poems included in the recently published anthologies *Eating Her Wedding Dress* and *In the Telling*.

IRA WOOD is the author of three novels, *The Kitchen Man, Going Public*, and *Storm Tide*, co-authored by Marge Piercy, with whom he has also written *So You Want to Write: How to Master the Craft of Writing Fiction and Memoir*. Together, they established Leapfrog Press, an internationally distributed "boutique" publishing company, which they sold in 2008. "You Are What You Owe" is a chapter from *The One Who Dies with the Most Sex Wins, and other Rules of DIStraction*, a recently completed memoir of linked stories.

BOOK REVIEWS
AT FWJ

In keeping with our mission of bringing a sharp readership together with the best storytellers and poets working today, *Fifth Wednesday Journal* is pleased to publish a book review section in every issue.

Literary books in all styles will be considered; however, an emphasis will be placed on the types of writing we publish in the journal, including short fiction, poetry, essays, and nonfiction works. Books devoted to black-and-white photography, either by one artist or several, also will be considered.

Publishers interested in having manuscripts reviewed by *Fifth Wednesday Journal* editors and writers should send inquiries on letterhead stationery to:

> Fifth Wednesday Books
> P.O. Box 4033
> Lisle, IL 60532-9033

Materials, including books and galleys, may be sent to:

> Daniel Libman
> Book Reviews Editor
> P.O. Box 67
> Oregon, IL 61061

FIFTH WEDNESDAY
JOURNAL

VACUUMING

Prairie Schooner

http://prairieschooner.unl.edu

We, too, dislike it.
Either the noise or the chore,
there's nothing to love.
Even nature abhors it.

So find someplace quiet, pick
up *Prairie Schooner*, and get
taken into the world of litera-
ture by the likes of Eudora
Welty, James Tate, Raymond
Carver, Pattiann Rogers,
Joyce Carol Oates, Honorée
Fanonne Jeffers, Cyrus Colter,
Minnie Bruce Pratt, Sherman
Alexie and the next literary
sensations.

Feed your heart and mind.
Let the dust bunnies gather
where they will. Join us today!

4 issues a year at $28.
Call 1-800-715-2387 with credit card
information or write
Prairie Schooner, 201 Andrews
Hall, University of Nebraska,
Lincoln NE 68588-0334

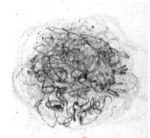

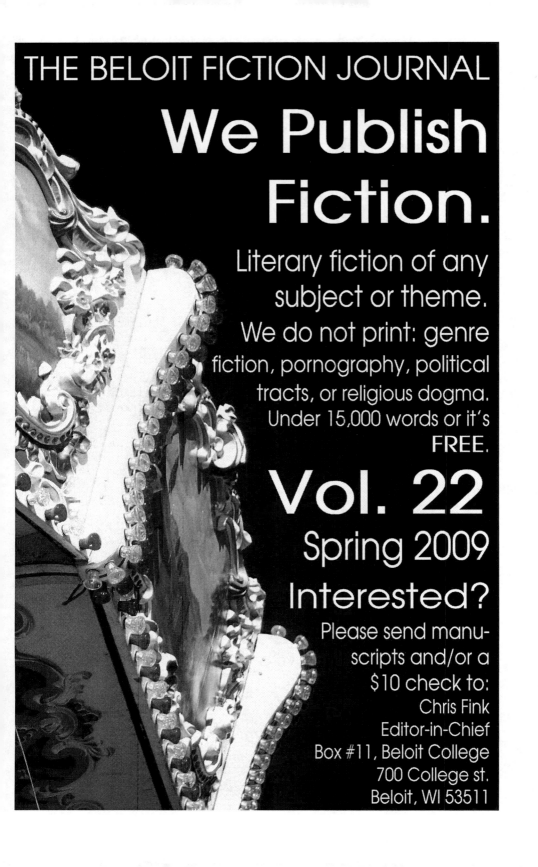

FIFTH WEDNESDAY
■ JOURNAL

Defining literature. In real context.
www.fifthwednesdayjournal.org

DONATION FORM

Donations may also be made online with a credit card at www.fifthwednesdayjournal.org/donate.

Donate to *Fifth Wednesday Journal* in three easy steps. Every dollar makes a difference!

▶ **CHOOSE YOUR DONATION LEVEL.**　　　　　　　　**AMOUNT**

☐ Up to $49 .... $_____

☐ $50-$499 – Special Friend .... $_____
Listing on the Patrons page in the magazine in the issue following your donation.

☐ $500-$999 – Special Reader .... $_____
Listing on the Patrons page in the magazine for two years with a complimentary lifetime subscription.

☐ $1,000 or more – Editors' Council .... $_____
Listing on the Patrons page in the magazine for three years with a complimentary lifetime subscription.

▶ **DESIGNATE THE PURPOSE OF YOUR GIFT.**　　　　　**AMOUNT**
(Choose one designation, or divide your gift among two or more funds.)

☐ Writers' Fund .... $_____

☐ Special Events Fund .... $_____

☐ Web Fund .... $_____

☐ General Operating Expenses *(default if none is indicated)* ...... $_____

TELL US WHO TO THANK! *(Your donations will be tax deductible to the fullest extent allowed by law. We will send you a receipt.)*
Your Name: _____
Your Address: _____

Whose name should we list on the Patrons page? *(For amounts of $50 or more.)*

☐ Please use my name as shown: _____
☐ List my donation in honor of: _____
☐ Keep my donation anonymous.

☐ Yes! I'd like to receive FWJ's e-mail updates.
E-mail:_____

Please mail this completed form with your check to:
Fifth Wednesday Books / P.O. Box 4033 / Lisle, IL 60532-9033

Questions? Please e-mail editors@fifthwednesdayjournal.org　　　　**Thank you!**

FIFTH WEDNESDAY
JOURNAL

Defining literature. In real context.
www.fifthwednesdayjournal.org

ORDER FORM

Orders may also be placed online with PayPal or credit card at www.fifthwednesdayjournal.org/order.

▶ SUBSCRIPTIONS	INSIDE THE U.S.	OUTSIDE THE U.S.	TOTAL
2 years (4 issues)	☐ $32	☐ $40	$____
1 year (2 issues)	☐ $17	☐ $21	$____

▶ SINGLE ISSUES
Quantities of 1–4 only*

	INSIDE	OUTSIDE	TOTAL
Fall 2009	____ x $10 (QUANTITY)	____ x $12 (QUANTITY)	$____
Spring 2009	____ x $10 (QUANTITY)	____ x $12 (QUANTITY)	$____
Fall 2008	____ x $10 (QUANTITY)	____ x $12 (QUANTITY)	$____
Spring 2008	____ x $10 (QUANTITY)	____ x $12 (QUANTITY)	$____
Fall 2007	____ x $9 (QUANTITY)	____ x $11 (QUANTITY)	$____

▶ T-SHIRTS

	INSIDE	OUTSIDE	TOTAL
XL	____ x $12 (QUANTITY)	____ x $15 (QUANTITY)	$____
L	____ x $12 (QUANTITY)	____ x $15 (QUANTITY)	$____
M	____ x $12 (QUANTITY)	____ x $15 (QUANTITY)	$____
S	____ x $12 (QUANTITY)	____ x $15 (QUANTITY)	$____

TOTAL AMOUNT INCLUDED WITH ORDER $ _____

SHIPPING INFO
Name: _____
Street Address: _____
City, State, ZIP: _____

☐ Yes! I'd like to receive FWJ's e-mail updates.
E-mail: _____

Please mail order with payment to:
Fifth Wednesday Books / P.O. Box 4033 / Lisle, IL 60532-9033

*For pricing of 5 or more copies, please e-mail editors@fifthwednesdayjournal.org.